THE COMPLETE

PC

UPGRADE & MAINTENANCE LAB MANUAL

SECOND EDITION

**RICHARD MANSFIELD
AND
EVANGELOS PETROUTSOS**

San Francisco • Paris • Düsseldorf • Soest • London

SYBEX

Publisher: Jordan Gold

Contracts and Licensing Manager: Kristine O'Callaghan

Acquisitions & Developmental Editor: Diane Lowery

Editor: Carol Henry

Production Editor: Nathan Whiteside

Technical Editor: Steve Wisniewski

Book Designer: Bill Gibson

Electronic Publishing Specialist: Franz Baumhackl

Proofreaders: Nanette Duffy, Andrea Fox, Amey Garber, Rodda League, Suzanne Stein

Cover Designer: John Nedwidek/emdesign

The authors dedicate this book
to Jim Coward

Acknowledgments

Above all, we credit Diane Lowery, developmental editor extraordinaire, for her consistently valuable guidance and advice during the entire process of bringing this book to the public. Diane is one of those (alas all too rare) editors who knows what's important and what's not—when to raise significant questions and also when to leave minor, purely subjective, style issues alone.

We also acknowledge Editor Carol Henry for her diligent and sensitive improvement of our original work. A good editor is quite valuable to both reader and writer, standing in the reader's stead—as the first reader of the work—and preventing confusion and embarrassment all around.

Technical Editor Steve Wisniewski aided us by ensuring that our information remained both timely and accurate. Finally, Nathan Whiteside served as an energetic and helpful guiding hand by both maintaining a schedule and demonstrating his good cheer and diplomatic skills when that schedule appeared to be in danger.

Contents

How to Use This Book   *vii*

Lab 1:   The Computer   1

Lab 2:   Starting the Computer   7

Lab 3:   Essential CMOS Backup   15

Lab 4:   The Tools and Work Area   21

Lab 5:   Opening the Case   27

Lab 6:   Cables and Connectors   31

Lab 7:   Disassembling the Computer   39

Lab 8:   The Central Processing Unit   47

Lab 9:   CMOS Setup   53

Lab 10: Replacing the Power Supply   61

Lab 11: Preventive Maintenance   65

Lab 12: Virus Protection   71

Lab 13: Adding Memory   79

Lab 14: The Hard Drive   87

Lab 15: Installing a Hard Drive   95

Lab 16: Formatting   101

Lab 17: Multiple Disk Partitions   107

Lab 18: Master/Slave Configurations   115

Lab 19: Dual-Booting   121

Lab 20: Keeping Hard Disks in Good Shape   127

Lab 21: General Backup Techniques   133

Lab 22: Diagnosing and Fixing Hard Disk Problems   139

Lab 23: Installing a SCSI Adapter   145

Lab 24: Installing a Video Board   151

Lab 25: Installing a CD-ROM, CD-RW, or DVD Drive   159

Lab 26: The Serial and Parallel Ports   165

Lab 27: Installing a Modem   175

Lab 28: Connecting to the Internet   179

Lab 29: Networking PCs   187

Lab 30: Installing a Sound Card   197

Lab 31: Handling I/O Address Conflicts   203

Lab 32: The Device Manager   209

Lab 33: Using the Add New Hardware Wizard   215

Lab 34: Troubleshooting Printers   221

Lab 35: Solving IRQ Problems   225

Lab 36: Solving Mouse and Keyboard Problems   231

Lab 37: Power Safety—Line Noise Protection and Battery Backup   235

Lab 38: General Troubleshooting   241

Lab 39: Notebook Upgrades   247

Lab 40: Building the Ultimate Computer   255

Appendix: Six Essential Upgrades   265

How to Use This Book

Our goal was to provide a manual to supplement and complement *The Complete PC Upgrade & Maintenance Guide,* the famous book by Mark Minasi. We've tried to demonstrate—using concrete, understandable "laboratory" assignments—how students can learn to repair and upgrade PCs. We trust that you'll find our efforts useful.

Each Lab in the manual ties into information in the Minasi book, so we suggest that you first review the "What to Read in the Book" references found in each chapter. Read the information referenced there to prepare yourself for completing the hands-on steps in the Lab, and then answer the Lab questions.

Required Equipment

At least a 486 Windows 95/98/2000 computer (Pentium preferred) that includes an IDE hard drive and a CD-ROM (or DVD) drive.

Support Equipment

- Serial mouse
- Keyboard
- Video card
- Printer
- Power supply
- IDE hard drive
- IDE CD-ROM drive (or, optionally, a DVD drive)
- Various cables and hardware fittings
- Sound card
- Floppy drive
- SCSI card
- Modem

Required Software

- DOS 6.*x*
- Windows 95, 98, or 2000

- ISP (Internet Service Provider) arrangement
- Video card driver
- Microsoft mouse driver
- Sound card driver
- Modem driver
- CD-ROM driver
- Printer driver

Required Tools and Supplies

- Phillips screwdriver
- Needle-nose pliers
- Antistatic wrist strap
- Flat-blade screwdriver
- Blank floppy diskettes

Lab 1: The Computer

Objectives for This Lab

Upon completion of this lab, you will be able to recognize all the external connections on your computer.

Hardware & Software Requirements

Hardware: A working PC computer

Software: None for this lab

What to Read in the Book

Chapter 1, *The Complete PC Upgrade & Maintenance Guide,* Mark Minasi, Sybex

Introduction

This lab will familiarize you with the external parts of the computer; you won't even turn on the computer for this lab. Your objective here is to learn the importance of documenting every new item and making diagrams. Most of you know how to connect keyboards and mice to your computer, and perhaps printers or other peripherals that are attached to the connectors on the back of the computer. Before attempting to resolve a problem with these or any other parts of the computer, you must document the hardware and know what devices you can connect.

On the front of the computer you'll will find the power switch and a reset button. On some computers the reset button is too obvious; on others it's a tiny button that's positioned so you can't press it accidentally. The more interesting parts—the connectors you use to attach the peripherals—are on the back of the computer.

First, take a look at the power plugs. There should be a plug for the power cord, and nearly all computers have a separate plug for powering the monitor. Notice that the monitor need not be powered by the computer's plug; you can plug it directly to a power outlet.

WARNING   In the following labs you'll be asked to disconnect the power cables. When you disconnect the power cable from the computer or any peripheral, you must disconnect it from the wall outlet as well. Always make sure that you don't leave unattached cables connected to a power source, such as the outlet on the wall or the monitor's power plug on the computer.

The most important connectors are the keyboard connector and the parallel and serial ports. The keyboard is connected to a round connector, usually marked with a keyboard icon. The mouse is connected to another round connector, the PS/2 port, or it may be connected to a serial port. The PS/2 port is a 6-pin round connector. If you attach a new keyboard to an old computer, there's a good chance that the keyboard cable's plug won't fit in the keyboard connector on the computer. You'll need a keyboard with a different plug at the end of its cable, or a special adapter that you can buy at any computer store.

Most computers have two serial ports on the back: One is a 9-pin connector and the other is a 25-pin connector. Both of these connectors are male (they have prongs). Another 25-pin connector is female (it has holes); this is the parallel port. Serial ports are used to connect to modems and mice. Parallel ports are used to connect to printers and any other device that requires a faster data transfer rate, such as Zip drives and other backup units. The difference between the two types of port is that serial ports transmit (or receive) one bit at a time, and parallel ports move data one byte at a time.

On computers with an internal modem, you'll see two RJ-11 (telephone) jacks, labeled Line and Phone (or Tel). To communicate with the modem, connect the phone line from the wall jack to the Line jack. If there is a phone connected to the same wall jack, connect it to the computer's Phone jack, so that you can use the phone when the computer is not connected to the Internet. On computers with an external modem, the modem is connected via a serial cable to a serial port, and the RJ-11 connectors are on the back panel of the modem.

If the computer has a sound card installed, you'll see two or three round connectors at the back, typically labeled Speaker, Microphone (usually Mic), and Line In.

The last connector to look for is a 15-pin female connector that looks like the serial port, but with pins arranged in three rows. This is the VGA (Video Graphics Array) port, where the monitor is connected.

Some high-end modern computers have two additional connectors: SCSI (Small Computer System Interface), pronounced "skuzzy," and USB (Universal Serial Bus). The SCSI connector, shown in Figure 1.1, is a 50-pin female connector to which you can attach devices designed specifically for this interface. SCSI devices are discussed in more detail in Lab 23. The USB connector (see Figure 1.2) is a new specification and isn't present on most computers manufactured before 1999. USB connectors can be used to connect multiple devices, similar to the SCSI ports. Eventually, USB ports will replace the serial port.

F I G U R E   1.1
F I G U R E   1.1   Connectors for external SCSI devices

F I G U R E   1.2   USB connector (in center)

The devices you'll most commonly find connected on a USB port are external CD-Rs (CD-Record-able), and advanced pointing devices and digitizers such as styluses. Nearly all computers made in the last two years have built-in USB ports, but you'll also find extension boards with a USB port. Theo-retically, one USB port can support up to 127 devices, but you may have to insert a USB hub to connect multiple devices to the same USB port. Not many USB compatible devices exist yet, and the available ones aren't extremely popular. Nevertheless, USB ports will soon replace both serial and parallel ports (probably after release of the final version of the USB 2.0 standard).

You may see one other connector that looks like a telephone jack but has eight pins and connects to a cable that's much thicker than the telephone cable. Or you may see a thick round cable connected to a round metal connector on the computer. In either case, this tells you that you have a computer connected to a local area network (LAN). This computer has a LAN adapter, or NIC (Network Inter-face Card), and the cable connects the computer to the rest of the network. If the computer is con-nected to a LAN through a cable ending in a telephone jack connector, you can safely remove the computer from the network. However, if the computer is connected to the network through two thick round cables (each one going to a different computer), you should ask the network administrator to disconnect the computer from the network. It's possible to isolate other computers from the network by disconnecting one of them, so be sure you won't disrupt the operation of the entire network to fix a single machine.

Exercise

To Examine the Computer's External Connections

1. Turn off the power and remove the power cable. If the monitor has a separate power cable, dis-connect it as well.

2. Label each cable connected to the back of your computer. Label them according to the name of the connector on the computer. If the computer's ports are not identified, use the name of the external device to which each cable is connected, so that you can reconnect them later.

3. Examine the connectors on the back of the computer and identify them.

4. If both the keyboard and the mouse are connected to PS/2 ports, switch them. Then turn on the computer and see if they still work.

5. If the computer is connected to a LAN, find out where the network cables go. If there are two cables connected to the network card, locate the other two computers they're connected to.

6. Reconnect all the cables to the back of the computer.

Lab 1

DATE _____ NAME _____

1. Is the mouse connected to a serial port or to a PS/2 port?

_____

_____

2. Describe the function of the serial and parallel ports and the types of devices we connect to these ports.

_____

_____

_____

_____

_____

3. Describe the advantages of a SCSI port compared with the serial and parallel ports.

_____

_____

_____

_____

_____

_____

4. On your computer, is the modem connected to a serial port, or is there an internal modem?

_____

_____

_____

_____

_____

Lab 2: Starting the Computer

Objectives for This Lab

Upon completion of this lab, you will know

1. What happens when you turn on your computer.

2. The various Windows start modes.

Hardware & Software Requirements

Hardware: A working PC computer with DOS and/or Windows 95/98

Software: None for this lab

What to Read in the Book

Chapter 3, page 151; Chapter 5, page 288; Chapter 7, pages 401–13, *The Complete PC Upgrade &*
Maintenance Guide, Mark Minasi, Sybex

Introduction

Computers don't usually die. They get sick and lose some data, or they can't see their hard drives, or
they fail to connect to the network; and that's when you'll be called on to fix them. More often than
not, a sick computer will not load the operating system from the drive successfully; it may not even recognize its hard drives or the CD-ROM drive. To fix a sick computer, you must understand what normally happens when you turn it on. This lab explains what happens when you start the computer in
DOS, Windows 3.1, or Windows 95/98. As you'll see, a lot of programs are loaded, and each one performs a specific task before you ever see the A:\ prompt (in DOS systems) or the Desktop (in Windows
systems).

The process of starting the computer is called *booting,* and a lot goes on when a computer is booted. The
programs that initialize the computer and test the various peripherals and their device drivers are quite
complex (although that isn't obvious, because they have little or no user interface). No matter what operating system you're using, it's the BIOS that initializes the computer every time you turn it on. The BIOS
is the most important software on your computer, in the sense that it tells the CPU how to communicate
with the peripherals (the hard disks, keyboard, and so on). The BIOS is the first program to be invoked.

It initializes the computer and it remains in memory. Every time the CPU needs to communicate with the user (through the keyboard, video board, etc.) or with the peripherals (hard disks, floppy drives), it uses the services of the BIOS.

The DOS Boot Sequence

1. The processor reads the BIOS from ROM and starts executing it. ROM is slower than RAM, and many manufacturers prefer to copy the BIOS into RAM memory, from where it can be read faster.

2. The BIOS performs a hardware test. Any errors at this point are signaled by a sequence of short and long beeps, because the BIOS hasn't yet initialized the video adapter. This is the Power On Self Test (POST).

3. The BIOS tests the lower memory, which is needed for the BIOS to work. If there's a problem with the lower memory, BIOS itself will crash and there's no recovery procedure—you must replace the first bank of memory and restart the computer.

4. The computer's BIOS relinquishes control to the BIOS of other devices in the computer. The video adapter, for example, has its own BIOS that must be loaded by the system BIOS. Its main function is to test and initialize the adapter. The same is true for the network cards. After the devices' BIOS execute, they return control to the computer's BIOS.

5. The BIOS displays the startup screen and checks the components it controls, such as the memory, disk drives, ports, and so on.

6. The BIOS displays a summary of the computer's configuration, but this screen disappears too quickly to study. If you want to review the computer's configuration, use the BIOS Setup screen (described in Lab 9). Or, if you're quick, you can press the Pause button while the information is displayed on the screen.

7. The BIOS loads the first sector of the bootable disk—the MBR (Master Boot Record)—and relinquishes control of the PC to the MBR (which is a very short program). The MBR invokes the DOS Boot Record (DBR) and passes control to it.

8. The DBR loads the IO.SYS and MSDOS.SYS files (MSDOS.SYS is DOS) and passes control to them. If these files are missing, then the terrifying Non-System Disk error is displayed. When this happens, you should boot from a disk and make the disk bootable again with the SYS command.

9. IO.SYS loads and executes CONFIG.SYS. This file contains statements that set the environment and load the required device drivers.

10. Then IO.SYS file loads COMMAND.COM, which is the DOS interpreter.

11. COMMAND.COM loads and executes the AUTOEXEC.BAT file. Then it displays the DOS prompt, reads the statements entered at the command line, and executes them.

NOTE Both CONFIG.SYS and AUTOEXEC.BAT load a bunch of drivers. Some drivers may fail without affecting the operation of the computer (but one of the peripherals may not work). Other drivers may terminate the booting process. Again, start the computer with a floppy and comment out one or more lines in the CONFIG.SYS and AUTOEXEC.BAT files until you isolate the driver that prevented the successful completion of the booting process. (To comment out a line in these two files, prefix it with the REM statement.)

The Windows 3.1 Boot Sequence

Windows 3.1 is not an operating system per se. It's a visual environment that uses DOS, so the Windows 3.1 boot sequence is the same as the DOS boot sequence with a few additional steps. The AUTOEXEC.BAT file contains the statement WIN, which starts Windows. When Windows loads, it processes a number of files with the extension .INI (called *configuration files*), which contain information about the input/output devices.

The Windows 95/98 Boot Sequence

The Windows boot sequence is a bit more complicated, but it, too, starts with the BIOS. After the BIOS completes the POST, the following actions take place:

1. MSDOS.SYS and IO.SYS are loaded and executed. Then the Windows startup screen is displayed.

2. Windows starts loading. First, it checks the Registry and, if it's valid, more Windows components are loaded in the memory.

3. Windows detects the hardware. If new hardware is found, Windows attempts to load the appropriate drivers.

4. The CONFIG.SYS and AUTOEXEC.BAT files (if they exist) are processed at this point by IO.SYS.

5. Finally, the processor switches to Protected mode, and it loads and executes WIN.COM.

6. As Windows comes on, it loads additional drivers, such as network and display drivers.

If Windows Won't Start

If Windows doesn't start, you should attempt to bring it up in Safe mode. To do so, press F8 immediately (within two seconds) when the Windows startup screen appears. The boot menu will be displayed, and you can select one of the following options:

```
1. Normal

2. Logged (\Bootlog.txt)

3. Safe Mode

4. Step-by-step confirmation

5. Command prompt only

6. Safe mode command prompt only
```

The first option starts Windows normally. The process is just the same as if you hadn't pressed F8 at startup.

The second option is also the same, but it logs information about each step of the process in the BOOTLOG.TXT file in the root folder. Use this Logged option to find the source of a problem that prevents Windows from starting normally. You can open the BOOTLOG.TXT file in the root directory to find out what device driver didn't load properly. There are two lines for each driver in the log file: The first line begins with Loading Device and the second one begins with LoadSuccess. If a device driver failed to load, there won't be a LoadSuccess line for this device.

When you boot in Safe mode, Windows 95 loads only the absolutely necessary device drivers. Even the resolution of the monitor is dropped to 640×480. If you can start Windows in Safe mode, it means that the problem is caused by one of the device drivers Windows loads. Safe mode is meant for troubleshooting only, because the computer is seriously crippled in this mode. No network connections are established, and the only peripherals recognized are the hard drives and CD-ROM drives. After the installation of new hardware or software, Windows may come up in Safe mode on its own.

If you have trouble starting Windows, select option 4 in the boot menu, Step-by-Step Confirmation. In this mode, Windows goes through the startup process as usual, but it displays the name of each driver it's about to load and each statement it's about to execute, and gives you a chance to cancel the action. If, for example, you suspect that a problem with a network card is preventing Windows from starting, don't let Windows load the associated device drivers. Press Y (or Enter) to load the driver, or N to skip it. Use this startup mode if you suspect that a certain device is failing, so that you can skip the drivers for the specific device only.

The CONFIG.SYS File

Most of the lines in the CONFIG.SYS file load device drivers—the programs that support various devices or add new capabilities to existing devices. The related lines of the CONFIG.SYS file begin with the statement DEVICE = followed by the name of the device driver.

Bugs in CONFIG.SYS can freeze the system (by loading an incorrect driver, for example). If after the installation of a new device the system doesn't start, you must try starting it with a minimum CONFIG.SYS file and see if that works. Then you can add more lines to the CONFIG.SYS file to load additional drivers, until you discover the name of the device driver that fails.

If the CONFIG.SYS contains a SHELL statement, the AUTOEXEC.BAT file should contain the matching SET COMSPEC statement. If not, the system will freeze.

The AUTOEXEC.BAT File

The AUTOEXEC.BAT file contains primarily names of executables that must be loaded before any other program. Most of these executables are TSR (Terminate and Stay Resident) applications. TSR applications are loaded in high memory and can be invoked, usually with a special keystroke, at any time and from within any application.

TSRs often prevent DOS applications from responding properly to the keyboard. When this happens, disable the TSR applications and reactivate them one at a time to see which one is causing the problem. To disable a statement from the AUTOEXEC.BAT file, insert the statement REM at the beginning of a line. For example, the following line installs the mouse driver:

```
MOUSE.COM
```

On many systems this line is commented out during Windows installation as follows:

```
REM    MOUSE.COM
```

Exercise

To Match Drivers to Their Devices

One of the most useful troubleshooting tools is to start Windows in the Step-by-Step Confirmation mode, so that you'll be in control of the drivers that will be loaded. The problem with this mode is that you have to know the names of the drivers needed by each device. Here are the steps to find those names:

1. In Control Panel, open the System icon's Properties dialog box and select the Device Manager tab. Choose an item in the list and click the Properties button.

2. When the Properties window of the selected device appears, select the Drivers tab and click the Driver File Details button. In this dialog box you'll see the names of the device drivers used by the selected device. Notice that not all the drivers are required; and some drivers may be used by other devices as well.

3. Write down the device drivers used by the major expansion boards in your system. If you ever have to start Windows without loading all the drivers, you'll need this list.

To Start Windows in Step-by-Step Confirmation Mode

1. Now restart Windows and press F8 after the BIOS messages appear on the screen.

2. When the boot menu appears, select option 4 (Step-by-Step Confirmation). As Windows starts, you'll be able to see which device drivers it attempts to load and in what order.

3. First, the system will ask your permission to process the System Registry. Press Enter (or Y) to let it process the Registry.

4. Then the system will ask your permission to process the CONFIG.SYS file. Press Y again and you'll be prompted as each line in the CONFIG.SYS is executed.

5. After processing the CONFIG.SYS file, Windows will process AUTOEXEC.BAT. Again, let Windows process the AUTOEXEC.BAT file and you'll see each line before it's actually executed.

6. The last line in AUTOEXEC.BAT is the statement WIN, which starts Windows. Here comes the important stuff.

7. First, Windows will give you a chance to load all the device drivers. Press N or Escape.

8. From now on, you'll be prompted for each device driver. Press Y or Enter to load the corresponding device. Press N or Escape to skip the file.

9. Try to identify as many device drivers as you can and match them to the appropriate devices. This is a difficult exercise, but with time you'll become familiar with the driver names. Also pay attention to names of the files copied to the Windows\System folder by the installation software when you install a new device.

Lab 2

DATE _____ NAME _____

1. What is a TSR?

_____

_____

_____

2. Which lines in the CONFIG.SYS and/or AUTOEXEC.BAT files load the CD driver?

_____

_____

_____

3. Where do you look to find the names of the files that are needed by a specific device?

_____

_____

_____

Lab 3: Essential CMOS Backup

Objectives for This Lab

Upon completion of this lab, you will be able to

1. Create a hard copy of the crucial CMOS boot information.

2. Restore CMOS boot information when it has been lost.

Hardware & Software Requirements

Hardware: A working PC computer with Windows 95/98 installed.

Software: None for this lab.

What to Read in the Book

Chapter 2, pages 40–42; Chapter 3, pages 222–24, *The Complete PC Upgrade & Maintenance Guide*, Mark Minasi, Sybex

Introduction

All PC-style computers since the venerable XT model have relied on *CMOS* (complementary metal oxide semiconductor) *memory*, a special memory chip containing important configuration information about the computer. Particularly important are the specifications about your CD-ROM, diskette, and hard drive(s). For example, CMOS configuration memory tells the computer where to look for the operating system when power is turned on. Should the machine be booted from the hard drive? Or should it boot from the floppy diskette? If there is no floppy inserted, the machine then attempts to boot from the hard drive. The order in which the drives are searched for boot information is called the *boot sequence.*

In most machines, the diskette in drive A is the first place checked to see if it is a boot disk. Checking drive A first is useful in case there's a problem with your hard drive. You can at least boot the computer from the A drive using a "rescue diskette" and perhaps solve the hard drive problem from there.

CMOS also contains the current time and date; usually any system password information; the default setting for Num Lock (on or off); any power management settings (for instance, automatically turning off the monitor or hard drives after a period of inactivity); and possibly other fundamental settings and preferences. The most important CMOS information, however, is the boot sequence and hard drive specifications. If that information is missing or incorrect, it's likely that the computer cannot boot and the operating system will not load.

CMOS information, however, is not kept in a ROM chip, because then you wouldn't be able to change any of that information. Instead, CMOS is kept in RAM, which allows you to change the date, install a new kind of hard drive, or otherwise modify CMOS information. RAM memory isn't permanent; it must have power to "remember" its information, and power is provided to the CMOS chip by a small battery. Most systems use nonrechargeable lithium batteries that are supposed to last 3–10 years. A few systems employ rechargeable NiCad batteries.

NOTE Sometimes people find they have to type in their configuration information each time they start their computer; when they power-down, the information is lost. However, they assume there's no problem with the battery *because the time and date remain correct.* Sounds reasonable—but it's wrong. The battery *is* the problem in this situation. It requires far more power to "remember" the system settings than to run a clock. Therefore, a weak battery will maintain the time and date but lose all the configuration data every time the computer is turned off.

WARNING Another common misunderstanding relating to the setup CMOS chip is believing that one of your disk drives has gone bad because it is identified as bad during setup. Drives *can* go bad, of course, but sometimes the CMOS simply contains the wrong information about the drive in question. If the CMOS battery goes dead, some computers proceed to boot up with default but incorrect settings for the hard drive. When the battery goes bad, CMOS reverts to the factory default settings which, for example, would be unaware that you have added a DVD drive. The solution to this problem is to enter your computer's Setup program to tell CMOS about your true hardware, and replace the battery while you're at it. Both of these tasks are described in Lab 9.

You should keep a copy of your CMOS information, for two very good reasons: The data might get lost when you're disassembling parts of your computer to replace or repair its components, or your battery might simply give out. If you have a written copy of the CMOS data, you can restore that data and get the computer up and running again very quickly. So if you turn on a computer and see this message:

```
Configuration information has been lost. Please restore the CMOS
information
```

it means you've lost the CMOS data. If you've got a hard copy of the CMOS information, all you need to do to solve this problem is enter the Setup mode and retype the information.

NOTE SCSI hard drives contain their own custom BIOS built right into the drives. They bypass that portion of the computer's setup devoted to hard drives, so if you use SCSI, your setup will report that no hard drives are attached to the machine, even though the SCSI drives do, in fact, exist.

Exercise

To Create a Hard-Copy Backup of CMOS Data

1. Turn on the computer, and press F2 at the very start of the boot process (before Windows 95/98 starts running). The Setup screen is displayed.

NOTE F2 is the most popular key today to get to Setup, but some machines might require that you press F1, F10, Ctrl+Alt+Esc, Ctrl+Alt+Ins, Del, or some other key or key combination. The required key (or combination) is usually displayed on the monitor when you first turn on your computer. If you don't see it, look at the documentation that came with the computer.

---

2. Setup screens feature various ways to access and edit their information, and most screens include a description of which keys you should press to move between the various data fields or turn to other "pages" of CMOS data. (Remember, you're not in Windows during boot-up, so the mouse is useless; even standard keys such as Page Up/Page Down might not behave as expected.) Locate the page that displays the hard-drive information. In some computers, the drive type will be provided (a number between 1 and 47).

3. Write down the hard-disk type (if provided), as well as the essential drive parameters: heads, cylinders, and sectors per track. If your drive is Type 47, that means "user-defined"; for this type, you must also write down the number of cylinders, sectors, and heads, the write-precompensation cylinder, and landing zone. In other words, with Type 47 you need to write down everything you see about each of your drives.

WARNING   Most contemporary computers include an auto-detect capability. This means the computer can figure out the details about its hard drive(s). As a result, vendors rarely, if ever, set new specific drive values—they let the BIOS do that job. When you turn on your machine, you can usually see the BIOS recognize each drive and display its vendor-specific information on the screen.

This process isn't perfect, however, so having a hard copy of those details is still a good idea. A few computers, though, do not permit the user to type in the hard-drive specifications. That information is *hard-wired* (cannot be modified by the user). The major advantage of the hard-wiring approach is that you never have to worry at all about losing this crucial information. But it also has a major disadvantage: It seriously limits the range of drives that can be used in such machines.

To Restore CMOS Settings

1. When you first turn on a computer, if you see some version of this message:

> Configuration information has been lost. Please restore the CMOS information

or this one:

> Invalid Hard Drive Type

or some other error message, press F2 (or whatever key or key-combination accesses Setup on your machine).

2. Using the hard copy you've just made of all the details about your hard drive(s), type in the specifications.

3. Save the CMOS data. (Use Ctrl+S or Esc, or whatever keys the Setup utility requires to store and save the information in the CMOS chip.)

4. Reboot the machine.

TIP   Symantec's Norton Utilities contains a utility that saves the CMOS information to a diskette. This diskette is called a *rescue diskette* and can be used to restore CMOS and other information to a crippled machine. See the documentation that comes with the Norton Utilities software.

Lab 3

DATE _____ NAME _____

1. Start your computer, and display the Setup screen that shows your hard drive(s) specifications. (Make a note of which keys you must press to access this information.) List the hard-drive specifications necessary to restore your computer's self-knowledge about its hard drive(s).

_____

_____

_____

_____

_____

_____

_____

2. What are the two most common events that are likely to cause CMOS data to be lost?

_____

_____

_____

_____

3. What does Setup report about SCSI drives, and where is the information about SCSI drives stored?

_____

_____

_____

_____

Lab 4: The Tools and Work Area

Objectives for This Lab

Upon completion of this lab, you'll be familiar with the tools you'll need to open the computer case and access the components inside.

Hardware & Software Requirements

Hardware:

1. An antistatic wrist strap

2. A set of screwdrivers

3. A nut driver

4. Needle-nosed pliers and diagonal cutters

5. Retrieving tools

6. A flashlight

7. A PLCC extractor

Software: None for this lab

What to Read in the Book

Chapter 2, pages 22–43, *The Complete PC Upgrade & Maintenance Guide*, Mark Minasi, Sybex

Introduction

Many computer problems are caused by software, and you'll be able to fix many apparent computer problems just by using the keyboard and the mouse. As a computer technician, you must understand the essentials of the system software and be able to configure the various devices, handle conflicts, and so on. Just consider how many times the average user's computer has to be fixed and how many times Windows has to be installed on top of an existing installation. Most computer problems today can be troubleshot without opening the computer case—without even turning the computer off—so a good understanding of the operating system and its tools is just as important as understanding the hardware parts.

Computer hardware fails, too; and you'll have to open the computer case, find the broken part, and replace it. The first rule in this area is, of course, don't fix it if it's not broken. Given that computers are getting more and more reliable, and considering that a major repair might cost more than a new motherboard, as a technician you'll be spending more time upgrading rather than fixing the computers in your care. Indeed, upgrading computers and building custom systems with many devices is no longer a task for the average user.

Before we look at the hardware tools that you need to open the case and access the computer's parts, let's discuss a few tools and practices for staying on top of general computer issues.

Staying Up-to-Date and Well Connected

Magazines, newsletters, and the Web are primary tools for your work, particularly as you focus on upgrading computers rather than fixing them. Follow the trade press, keep up to date on technology, and be ready to offer advice. Just knowing that a certain device doesn't work with a specific computer, or knowing about the special software needed to make it work, can save you many hours of tedious trial and error. Being able to suggest hardware that won't be quickly outdated is just as important.

The Internet is the ultimate source of information. Select Web sites with the most useful information for your environment and bookmark them. If a device doesn't work, don't automatically assume it's broken. Visit the manufacturer's site and find out if the hardware requires any special software or installation procedure. Subscribe to newsgroups, where you may find answers to many of your questions. If the information isn't already there, you'll be able to post questions and some of your peers may have the answers. With these sources, you'll be able to provide suggestions and information to others, and share with them your own experience with specific hardware. In newsgroups, the feedback is not immediate, but it's likely that you'll be posting questions about problems you've given up on anyway. Once you've reached that point, you can afford to wait another day or two!

Another solution is to address questions to the manufacturer of the device you're having problems with, through an appropriate Web site. Once you're connected to the manufacturer's site, look for a link that says "E-Mail Us," "Contact Us," "Technical Support," or something similar. Many sites respond through an automated system (they look for keywords in your message and send all documents that relate to those keywords). Give it a try and see if you can find sites that are helpful.

Trade shows are another invaluable source of information. They give you the chance to network with your peers and establish professional relationships, in addition to learning about the latest trends. And you'll often meet the people who can provide definite answers to your questions. If the person at a booth can't help you directly, ask for the name and phone number of someone who might have the answer. Once you have access to the designers of the computer or device, make sure you ask valid, nontrivial questions. At least make sure you've exhausted any help you can get from the 800 technical-support number before calling the insiders.

The Tools of the Trade

Now we're ready to look at the tools you'll be using to access the parts of your computer. The right tools will simplify your life and help you minimize the risk of destroying a chip—or even the motherboard. You may think you can take the computer apart and put it together again with a Swiss Army knife, and you're probably right—but the next person to work on the computer will probably notice it. No professional should be without the proper tools for doing the job right.

Antistatic Wrist Strap

The first truly essential tool you must buy is an antistatic wrist strap. Static electricity, which we generate all the time but don't feel unless the weather is really dry, can easily damage chips. The antistatic strap gets attached to your wrist on one end, and on the other end is an alligator clip that you attach to the computer's chassis to ground the strip. Be sure to attach the clip to the metal and not a plastic part of the case! Today's motherboards are less susceptible to static electricity, but you should make wearing the antistatic wrist strap a habit anyway. Make it a part of your ritual before you open a computer.

When you have to work on a computer unexpectedly and you don't have your antistatic strap handy, touch the computer's metal case before you touch the motherboard or any other part. Continue touching the metal case as often as possible to adequately discharge the static electricity. If the weather is dry or you're wearing wool, you may actually feel the shock as your body discharges on the metal case. This little shock can't hurt you, but it can easily damage chips.

Set of Screwdrivers

Most computer parts are held in place with screws, so you'll need a good set of screwdrivers. You'll need both standard (flat-edged) and Phillips (with an X-shaped tip to fit screws with two vertical edges) screwdrivers at various sizes. Because there are various sizes of screws, you can also buy a switching screwdriver that has several interchangeable tips that fit on a single handle. The tips can be either normal or Phillips. For some computers you may need a Torx screwdriver (a screwdriver with a six-sided, star-shaped head), so keep T-10 and T-15 Torx screwdrivers in your lab.

Perhaps the most useful screwdriver is one that's battery powered. Not only is this more convenient to work with (you don't have to balance the screwdriver on top of the screw as you turn it), but it applies the proper pressure, too. Some technicians use excessive force when they fasten screws manually, which may destroy the head of the screw. By the way, if the screwdriver won't fit into the screw's cuts, you can use a nut driver (see next section).

WARNING   For most noncomputer work, magnetic screwdrivers are very convenient; and chances are you have a few in your toolkit. *But do not use them when you work with your PC.* The magnet can cause all kinds of problems when brought near the internals of the PC and the diskettes.

Nut Drivers

A nut driver is a screwdriver with a hexagonal head that fits on top of the screw. This tool will come in very handy when you come across a screw with a stripped slot. Nearly all hexagonal screws are ¼" in diameter, so you'll need a ¼" nut driver. If you have an electric screwdriver, you can buy nut-driver attachments for it.

Needle-Nosed Pliers and Diagonal Cutters

The needle-nosed pliers are used to hold screws in places that are hard to reach—and there are many such places in a computer case, especially older ones. These pliers are also handy for pulling the jumper covers, especially when there are many jumpers positioned close together.

Another useful tool is the diagonal cutter. It's similar to the needle-nosed pliers, but instead of grippers it has a pair of diagonal cutters. You won't use it often, but when you come across a bundle of cables with a cable tie, the diagonal cutter is the only tool that will cut the cable tie in place.

Retrieving Tool

A retrieving tool has a button at the top and three small fingers at the other end. The button is connected to the fingers with a spring, and when you push the button the fingers spread apart. You then center the three fingers over the object that you want to pick up (usually a screw) and then release the button. The fingers contract and grab the object. If you've ever had to turn an entire computer case upside down and shake it to recover a wayward screw that's out of reach (sometimes out of sight, too), you know how useful this tool can be. Some retrieving tools have a flexible shaft to reach awkward places.

Flashlight

Hardly any toolkit is complete without a flashlight. In addition to hard-to-reach places inside a computer case, you'll encounter hard-to-read labels, too. If you don't want to remove half the parts in the computer case just to read a label, have a flashlight handy. A flexible flashlight can be very useful, too. For labels in especially hard-to-reach places, you may even want to keep a dental mirror on hand.

PLCC Extractors

This tool fits around a PLCC (Plastic Leadless Chip Carrier) and allows you to extract PLCC chips. Those chips are hard to get out without help, and you'll need the PLCC extractor when you have to upgrade a PLCC-type CPU. The other type of CPU, the PGA (Pin Grid Array), uses a so-called zero insertion force (ZIF) lever. This makes it very easy to insert and remove the CPUs on the special socket, and you won't need an extractor for this type of chip.

Exercise

To Prepare Your Work Area

1. Move a computer to your working place. Make sure you have access to enough outlets to power the unit and the monitor. Also make sure that the power cables are not stretched.

2. Find a multiple-outlet power strip. Some devices may have to be powered separately, such as tape drives and printers.

3. Before you open the computer case, you must *unplug all power cables* from the back of the computer and the peripherals. Obviously, you have to unplug them from the power outlet too; if you don't, you're risking electrocution. A multiple-outlet power strip with an On/Off switch will allow you to disconnect all power cables with the flip of a switch.

To Explore the Tools

1. Find out how the retrieving tools work. Try to pick up a few screws with the retrieving tool. Place a screw between two books or two boxes and try to lift it with the tool without touching the other objects.

2. Locate an old or unused expansion board (preferably a video graphics board) and try to extract a chip with a flat screwdriver. Notice that most of the chips are soldered on the motherboard. These chips can't be removed without a soldering iron. Only chips seated on a chip socket can be lifted out of a board or from the motherboard.

3. To remove a chip that's not soldered (most older video boards have two socketed ROM chips), select a flat screwdriver that will fit between the chip and its socket. Do not try to extract the chip in a single step. If you pull one of the sides totally out of the socket, the legs that are still in the socket will bend. Begin by inserting the screwdriver slowly and lifting slightly on one side of the chip.

4. Then do the same with the other end of the chip.

5. Repeat steps 3 and 4 until the chip has been extracted completely.

6. If you've bent the legs by mistake, bend them back to their vertical position with the needle-nosed pliers.

7. Find an old computer and loosen the screws that hold the cover on the chassis. Select the proper size screwdriver for the screws.

8. When the screws are loose, screw them back in with the same screwdriver. Tighten the screws to a snug fit, but don't use excessive force.

9. If you have a nut driver, repeat steps 7 and 8 with the nut driver (provided that the screws have hexagonal heads, of course).

Lab 4

DATE _____ NAME _____

1. Identify each tool by name.

_____

_____

_____

_____

2. Is it all right to use magnetic screwdrivers to pick up small metal objects (like screws) from inside the computer case?

_____

_____

3. What's the best tool for extracting screws?

_____

_____

_____

Lab 5: Opening the Case

Objectives for This Lab

Upon completion of this lab, you will be able to

1. Remove a desktop computer's case.

2. Remove a tower computer's case.

Hardware & Software Requirements

Hardware:

1. A PC tower or desktop computer

2. A Phillips screwdriver or nut driver

Software: None for this lab

What to Read in the Book

Chapter 2, pages 43–46, *The Complete PC Upgrade & Maintenance Guide*, Mark Minasi, Sybex

Introduction

After you've backed up your CMOS (see Lab 3), the next step when upgrading or replacing an internal component is opening the computer's case. This used to be an unpleasant job, involving typically four screws (for a desktop model) or six screws (for a tower model). However, some current computers have been designed to make life easier for all of us. They require only that you use your fingers to unscrew a single knob (a thumbscrew). In other current models, all you do is press a button on the front of the computer and, voilá, you can lift off the case.

In this lab, we'll tackle the more difficult, older, screw-style case. Removing the modern cases is usually a snap.

Exercise

To Remove a Typical Desktop Computer's Case

1. Turn off the power switch on the computer, and turn off the power to all peripherals.

2. Unplug the computer.

3. Using either a screwdriver or nut driver, remove the screws that hold the cover in place. They are the outermost screws, the screws on the lip of the case itself, as you can see in Figure 5.1.

WARNING   Do not unscrew the screws that are not located on the outer case.

F I G U R E   5.1   The location of the case screws on a typical desktop computer

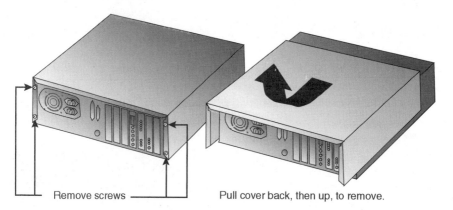

Remove screws ———————   Pull cover back, then up, to remove.

4. Put the screws in a safe place so you can reassemble the case later.

TIP   If you lose some of the case screws, replace them with type 6-32, 3/8" hex head/Phillips screws. *Each* screw serves a structural purpose—so don't get lazy and leave some of the screws off when you reassemble the case.

5. Carefully pull the cover a few inches back toward the rear of the computer, and then pull up to remove (see Figure 5.1).

WARNING   It's very easy to scratch or even tear the fragile ribbon cables inside the computer if you remove the cover too quickly. *And be warned:* Even a slightly scratched ribbon cable can cause its attached disk drive to behave badly or fail.

To Remove a Typical Tower Computer's Case

1. Follow steps 1 through 3 of the foregoing exercise "To Remove a Typical Desktop Computer's Case," but in step 3 remove all screws or thumbscrews.

2. Put the screws in a safe place so you can reassemble the case later.

3. Carefully pull the cover a few inches back toward the rear of the computer, and then pull up to remove. The difference between this step and step 5 in the preceding exercise is that a tower-style computer stands vertically, and you pull the case off in its normal, vertical position.

Lab 5

DATE _____ NAME _____

1. What important step should you take involving your CMOS before removing the case?

_____

_____

_____

2. Does it matter if you leave out a screw or two when putting the case back on the computer?

_____

_____

_____

3. Why should you remove the computer's case slowly?

_____

_____

_____

4. How can you tell the difference between the screws that secure the case and the other screws that hold components such as the power supply?

_____

_____

_____

Lab 6: Cables and Connectors

Objectives for This Lab

Upon completion of this lab, you will be able to

1. Recognize the various cables in your PC.

2. Identify the most important connectors on the motherboard.

3. Identify the switches and jumpers on the motherboard.

Hardware & Software Requirements

Hardware:

1. A working PC computer

2. A Phillips screwdriver or nut driver

3. An antistatic wrist strap

4. A voltage meter

Software: None for this lab

What to Read in the Book

Chapter 2, pages 46–51, 56, and 66–68; Chapter 6, pages 330–32; *The Complete PC Upgrade & Maintenance Guide,* Mark Minasi, Sybex

Introduction

You now know how to open the computer's case, and you're probably eager to take your PC apart. You'll do that in the next lab. But first, you must familiarize yourself with the cables stashed in the computer and their connectors.

The motherboard contains the CPU, memory, and other support circuitry. Other crucial parts of the computer, like the drives, are not incorporated on the motherboard. These parts communicate with the CPU on the motherboard through the bus and special cables. The same parts must also be powered, and many of the wires in the computer's case are used to power the drives and other devices.

The motherboard contains a few switches, which allow you to configure the hardware. These switches are the jumpers and DIP (dual in-line package) switches. A *jumper* is a pair of metal prongs, and you turn it on by shorting the two prongs with a small cover. DIP switches come in two forms: rocker switches and slide switches. These switches are shown in Figure 6.1.

F I G U R E 6.1 Typical DIP switches

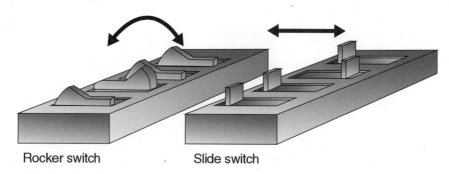

Rocker switch   Slide switch

Data Cables

The flat cables that come out of the drives and end in some connector either on the motherboard or an expansion board are called *ribbon cables* or *data cables*. These cables are used to move data to and from the peripherals, similar to the serial and parallel cables you use to connect external devices to the computer. At the very least, you will find two ribbon cables: one that connects the motherboard to the floppy drive(s), and another one that connects the motherboard to the hard drive(s) and the CD-ROM drive.

Sometimes you may have to unplug these cables to access hard-to-reach places in the case. Before you unplug a cable, make sure you can put it back again correctly. Notice that each ribbon cable's first (or last) wire is colored differently; it is usually red or striped. This wire corresponds to pin 1. If this pin is labeled on the connector, it's easy to plug in the ribbon cable again. If the connector's first pin isn't labeled, write down the orientation of the colored wire (for example, "to the side of the case" or "the leftmost pin when viewed from the top") so that you will know how to plug the cable back into its connector.

TIP If you insert a hard drive's data cable backwards, nothing fatal will happen to the drive. When you turn on the computer, however, the light on the drive will remain on and the drive won't work. If this happens, you must open the case, unplug the drive's connector, and reconnect it.

Each ribbon cable has two connectors attached to it. This means you can connect two drives to the same controller on the motherboard. Nearly every modern motherboard has two 40-pin connectors for hard drives (for a total of four hard drives) and one 34-pin connector for floppy drives (for a total of two floppy drives). The connectors on the hard drives' ribbon cables are the IDE/EIDE connectors shown in Figure 6.2, and Figure 6.3 shows the floppy drive's cable with its connectors.

F I G U R E 6.2   A ribbon cable connecting multiple hard drives

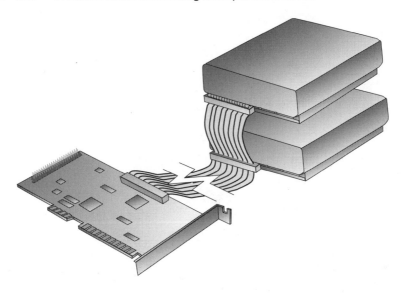

F I G U R E 6.3   A floppy drive cable and its connections

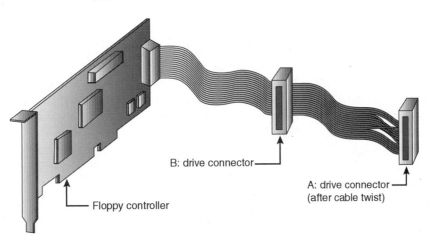

B: drive connector

A: drive connector
(after cable twist)

Floppy controller

You'll notice that not all the connectors on a ribbon cable are connected to a drive or other peripheral. Mark these "orphan" connectors accordingly, so that you won't be tempted to insert them anywhere later.

Power Cables

The power supply provides the power needed by all the components of the computer to operate. The power cables are easy to distinguish because they consist of four colored wires. Each wire carries a different voltage, as summarized in the following tables. Here are the voltages for power wires on AT motherboards:

Wire Color	Rated Voltage	Acceptable Range
Yellow	+12 volts	+8.5 to +12.6 volts
Blue	−2 volts	−8.5 to −12.5 volts
Red	+5 volts	+2.4 to +4.2 volts
White	−5 volts	−4.5 to −5.4 volts
Black	Ground	

The newer ATX power supplies have a few additional wires:

Wire Color	Rated Voltage	Indicator
Brown	Sense +3.3 Volts	
Gray		Power OK
Green		PS-ON
Purple	5-VSB	

On these ATX power supplies, when the Power OK wire is on, it indicates that the power is good. The PS-ON wire is used by Windows to soft-control the power and shut off the computer even when you don't press the power button. Finally, the 5-VSB wire is a standby voltage source that can power the circuits when power is off. That's how some systems can be started by pressing a special key. The keyboard isn't connected to the power supply, but a special circuit monitors the status of the Power key and they start the computer when this key is pressed.

The power supply provides multiple cables, which end in either a Molex or a Berg connector. The Molex connectors are used to power the hard drives; the smaller Berg connectors are used with the floppy drives. The unused power connectors can be left lying inside the computer case, as long as they're not near any jumpers or other metal pins.

Exercise

To Become Familiar with the Motherboard Connections

1. Turn off the computer, unplug all external cables, and open the case.

2. Notice that the ribbon cable connecting the floppy drive(s) to the motherboard is twisted between the two connectors. The drive that goes to the end connector (after the twist) is drive A. The drive connected to the connector before the twist is drive B.

3. Swap the connector on floppy drive A. If the computer has two floppy drives, you can leave drive B unconnected. When you restart the computer, floppy drive A will become B and vice versa.

4. Plug in the power cable (as well as any other cables and expansion boards you may have removed) and turn on the computer. Do not close the computer's case yet.

5. When the computer comes on, verify that the drive names were swapped.

6. Turn off the computer and restore the connection(s) to the floppy drive(s). Notice the original arrangement of the floppy drives in their bays. This arrangement simplifies the connection of the two drives to the ribbon cable.

7. Locate all the cables that come out of the power supply. These are four-wire cables that end in Molex or Berg connectors and are used to power the motherboard and the drives.

8. Write down the devices to which the power cables are connected. Most devices that draw power from the computer's power supply have a single connector for the power cable. Some devices may have both a Molex and a Berg connector. In this case, you can use either connector, but not both of them.

9. Locate a cable wire that ends in a Molex or Berg connector and is not used to power any device. Make sure that all other cables are in place, and then turn on the computer.

10. Use a meter to read the voltage between the first and second wires of the connector.

11. Then read the voltage between the yellow, red, blue, and white wires against the black (ground) wire. The values of the voltage between a colored wire and the ground should be +/−12 volts and +/−5 volts, approximately.

12. Write down the colors of the wires in each pair and the voltage value that you measured.

13. The jumpers on the motherboard are usually grouped together. Consult the motherboard's documentation to find out what each jumper (or group of jumpers) does.

14. Locate all the DIP switches on the motherboard and write down their names (or locations, if they have no names) and the settings of the individual switches. If the On/Off positions are not marked on the motherboard, make an arbitrary decision, write it down, and use it to document the settings of the DIP switches. You can also consult the motherboard's documentation and infer the On/Off positions from the current settings.

15. Change the setting of a DIP switch and then change it back to its original position by sliding its button (or pressing the switch of a rocker switch).

16. Change the setting of a jumper and then change it back to its original setting. To turn a jumper off, you simply remove the special cover on top of one or both prongs. When you turn a jumper off, do not remove the cover. Just fit it over one of the prongs, so that it will be there the next time you open the computer.

Lab 6

DATE _____ NAME _____

1. How many IDE/EIDE and floppy connectors are in your computer? How many of these connectors are used?

_____

_____

_____

2. How many of the connectors on the ribbon cables are used? List the additional drives you can add to your computer.

_____

_____

_____

_____

_____

_____

3. List all the devices that are powered by a four-wire power connector.

Molex connectors:

_____

_____

_____

Berg connectors:

_____

_____

_____

4. Draw a diagram of the motherboard, showing the power cables, data cables, and the DIP switches and jumpers on the motherboard. You need not draw everything you see on the motherboard—just a few characteristic connectors, the power supply, and the CPU. Represent the drives with little boxes and draw lines to represent the connections to the motherboard.

Lab 7: Disassembling the Computer

Objectives for This Lab

Upon completion of this lab, you will be able to

1. Disassemble the computer.

2. Put it back together.

Hardware & Software Requirements

Hardware:

1. A working PC computer

2. An antistatic wrist strap

3. A Phillips screwdriver

Software: None for this lab

What to Read in the Book

Chapter 2, *The Complete PC Upgrade & Maintenance Guide,* Mark Minasi, Sybex

Introduction

Disassembling the computer is probably the one thing you'll become an expert at. You may find that you cannot fix every problem or perform every desired upgrade, but you must still be able to take the computer apart before you can even try repairing or upgrading it. The first rule is to use an antistatic wrist strap. Most users occasionally replace a memory module without the wrist strap, but don't take any chances. If you don't have a wrist strap, touch a metal part on the computer's case before you handle anything on the motherboard or even the computer's hard drives.

Before you open the computer's box, be sure to do the following:

1. Collect all the documentation on the computer and its components (expansion boards, monitor, and so on). If you open a relatively modern computer to upgrade it, rather than fix it, you'll usually find all the information you need in the documentation. Compare your motherboard to the drawing in the documentation, and identify the connectors and cables on your motherboard.

2. Locate the warranty and make sure the computer *isn't* under warranty. If it is, you should probably take it back to the vendor, or ship it there. You may invalidate the warranty by fixing it yourself, not to mention that some vendors have a 24-hour turnaround service policy; some of them may even loan you another computer for the duration of the service. When vendors service their own computers, they will often replace the motherboard with a new one, even if this isn't absolutely necessary—sometimes, it costs less to replace than to troubleshoot.

NOTE By the way, you should also have a boot diskette at hand, because you may not be able to boot the computer from the hard drive.

During the process, you may discover that things are a little different on your computer than what we describe here. For the most part, however, the items described and their locations should be the same. Make sure you'll be able to place everything back into its original position when you're done. Most cables can't be placed backwards and can only be attached to one connector. This isn't a rule, however, and you can damage the motherboard by swapping the order of the two cables that power it (for example).

Before you start working with your computer, have plenty of room on your desk for the machine and the parts you will remove. As you remove screws, place them in separate lots. This will make it easier to find the original screws for each component (the screws for the case, the power supply, and so on) when you put everything back together.

It's nearly impossible to describe all the parts you may find in every computer you'll open. If you have access to different computers, you should attempt to disassemble them all.

WARNING Stay clear of disassembling notebooks. Without the proper training, there's very little you can do with notebook computers beyond adding memory or replacing a hard disk drive according to the manufacturer's instructions. Lab 40 shows you how to perform simple upgrades to notebook computers.

Exercise

To Disassemble the Computer

1. Turn off the PC and all peripherals, disconnect all cables, and remove the computer's cover (see Lab 5 for details).

2. Once you can see the motherboard, write down the location and settings of all DIP switches and jumpers. You should also diagram the cables and their connections to the motherboard and expansion boards. While you're documenting the cables and connectors, write down the connectors that have no cable on them—so that you won't be tempted to plug any of the free cables into these connectors when you reassemble the computer.

3. Remove all the expansion circuit boards from their slots, as explained in the following step. Identify each board and write down the slot it came from. If any of the boards have cables attached to them, write down which cable goes where, as well as the orientation of the cable (use the cable's colored wire and the Pin 1 Rule as a guide). Some connectors are completely symmetrical, and it's possible to insert the cables the wrong way. If needed, attach small labels to the cables so that you can easily identify them and their orientation.

4. To remove a circuit board, remove the board's mounting screw and then pull the board out of the slot. Some boards aren't easy to pull, so you may have to rock them a little. Move the board back and forth, *not* side-to-side. Most boards include a metal brace that attaches to the case. That's why it's imperative to unplug all the cables before you open the case.

5. Disconnect all cables that come out of the power supply. If there are two connectors powering the motherboard, they end up in the sockets P8 and P9 on the motherboard. Make sure you mark the cables that go into each connector. If you put them in backwards when you reassemble the computer, you'll destroy the motherboard. The power cables' Molex connector has one rounded corner only, so it can't be inserted the wrong way.

6. Label all the flat cables connecting the drives to the motherboard or to a circuit board. Then write down where each cable goes, as well as the orientation of the red wire. One of the end wires of the flat cable is colored red; write down the side of the connector on the drive that corresponds to the colored wire ("upper-right corner," "lower-left," and so on). If you can't see the colored wire, then color one of them, or draw an arrow on the ribbon cable pointing to one of the two end wires. This will be your colored wire, which isn't necessarily the red wire discussed in the book. Describe on paper the orientation of the cable with respect to the connector to which your red wire is connected—before you remove the cable.

7. The flat cables have two connectors on them. Write down which connector goes to each drive.

8. Remove the flat cables from the drives.

9. Remove all drives from their bays (but not before you write down their original locations). To do so, locate the screws that hold the drive to the case. Each drive is held in place by four screws, two on each side. Then pull out the drive slowly. Some drives must be pulled from the inside; other must be pushed outward. Technically, the order of the drives in the bays isn't important, as long as they're connected to the proper cables. If you switch their order, however, it may be more difficult to fit them back in, because of crossing cables.

10. Remove the power supply. To do so, remove the screws that hold it to the case. Be sure to hold the power supply as you remove the last screw and the power supply comes free, so that it doesn't fall on the motherboard. If the power switch is located on the front of the computer, it is a software-driven switch, which is used with Advanced Power Management (APM) PCs and is connected to the motherboard with two small wires. Diagram the connection and remove the wires. If there are four thick wires going to the front switch, then you have an actual power switch. Do not remove these wires unless you have diagrammed their connections. Make a mistake here and you're sure to fry your motherboard. Depending on the design of the computer, it may be possible to remove the switch along with the power wires. Be sure to understand how the power wires are attached to the power switch. All this is described in detail on pages 62–64 of *The Complete PC Upgrade & Maintenance Guide*.

11. Spend some time examining the various boards and the drives. Write down the information printed on the hard drive regarding its capacity, heads, and cylinders.

To Reassemble the Computer

1. Now you must put everything together again and make a working computer. Start by screwing the power supply onto the chassis, and then connect the power cables to the motherboard and the power switch.

2. Insert the drives in their bays and screw them on. Then connect the power and data cables according to the diagrams you have made. If you're not sure how a cable is oriented (ribbon cables are symmetric and can be inserted the wrong way), use the Pin 1 Rule described on pages 66–68 of *The Complete PC Upgrade & Maintenance Guide*. If the ribbon cables are in the way of the expansion boards, you should swap steps 2 and 3 in this exercise.

TIP Notice that ribbon cables can be inserted even if they're offset by one pin or by an entire row. Their sockets aren't designed to prevent this misalignment, so be extra careful when inserting ribbon cables in their sockets, especially in hard-to-see places. This is where you may need a flexible flashlight and/or a dental mirror. If needed, feel the socket around the cable with your fingers to make sure the cable was inserted perfectly in the connector—if the cable was misaligned, you'll feel the part of the connector that is empty.

3. Reinsert the boards in their slots and make sure they're seated firmly. You don't actually have to place the boards in their original slots; but if you don't, the connectors on the back of the computer will have a different arrangement. The *only* good reason for moving boards around is to get some wires out of the way. You must also make sure that each board fits in the slot before attempting to insert it there. On most computers, you'll find two different types of slots; each board fits into one type of slot but not both.

4. Finally, close the computer case, connect all external cables (power cables, monitor and printer cables, and so on), and turn on the computer.

Lab 7

DATE _____ NAME _____

1. How many drives are in the computer? Describe how they're connected to the motherboard and power supply.

_____

_____

_____

_____

_____

_____

_____

_____

2. Are the computer's serial and parallel ports on a separate board, or are they on the motherboard?

_____

_____

_____

_____

3. Describe how you would insert a ribbon cable into its connector.

_____

_____

_____

_____

_____

4. Describe the function of the four wires that go from the power supply to the front panel switch.

_____

_____

_____

_____

_____

_____

Lab 8: The Central Processing Unit

Objectives for This Lab

Upon completion of this lab, you will be able to replace the CPU (Central Processing Unit) in your computer with a faster one.

Hardware & Software Requirements

Hardware: A working PC computer

Software: None for this lab

What to Read in the Book

Chapter 3, pages 76–138, *The Complete PC Upgrade & Maintenance Guide*, Mark Minasi, Sybex

Introduction

The CPU is the heart of the PC, and its performance affects the overall performance of the computer more than any other component. The speed of the CPU is determined by the rate of an internal clock, and the higher the clock rate, the faster the CPU works. Unfortunately, you can't make your computer run faster by raising the clock rate. CPUs are designed to work at specific clock rates. If the rate of the clock is raised beyond a certain limit, the CPU will no longer function properly, and under no circumstances should you attempt to overclock the CPU. If a computer is unstable, run the BIOS Setup program to find out if the CPU has been overclocked.

There are many types of CPUs out there and many of them are already obsolete. Computers are still in use that have 80286 and 80386 processors, and you won't be able to upgrade these processors simply because you can't buy a faster 80286/80386 processor. Even slower Pentiums (machines that run at clock rates of 166 MHz or less, for example) are hard to find. This lab assumes that you are replacing a Pentium CPU with a faster one. A Pentium running at 75MHz is considered very slow nowadays and can probably be replaced with a Pentium at 90 or 120MHz. Perform this upgrade if the original CPU has failed, and go for the fastest CPU of the same type that the motherboard will accommodate. Nevertheless, upgrading a 90MHz Pentium with another one that runs at 120MHz to improve performance will yield only marginal improvements, and you should consider replacing the entire motherboard. New motherboards are not very expensive and they'll go a long way. Lab 40 gives information on replacing the motherboard.

When you upgrade the CPU, go for the fastest rate the motherboard can accommodate. You'll find this information in the motherboard's documentation. Most likely you'll have to set some jumpers on the motherboard to specify the speed of the new CPU. The documentation contains a list of processors and speeds supported by the motherboard and the corresponding settings of some of its jumpers. If you can't find the documentation, call the manufacturer.

TIP Some Pentium processors come with their own fan or heat sink. When you purchase a processor, ask whether you should buy a fan as well. If the CPU comes in an SEC (Single Edge Cartridge) package, you don't need a separate fan. (Figure 3.4 in *The Complete PC Upgrade & Maintenance Guide* shows a Pentium CPU in an SEC package.)

Many older 486 and Pentium systems accept an Overdrive chip. This chip either replaces the original CPU, or fits into a separate Overdrive socket on the motherboard and takes over the original CPU. If you go for an Overdrive chip, make sure the motherboard can accept it; and find out whether it requires specific jumper settings.

The Pentium CPUs use two clocks: an internal clock and the external computer clock. The external clock is that of the motherboard, and it's pretty slow compared to the CPU's internal clock. The fastest motherboards today run at 133MHz and will, most likely, support the 1GHz CPUs you may see early in 2001. Making a fast motherboard is considerably more complicated (and more expensive) than making a faster CPU. The internal clock is two, three, four, or five times as fast as the external clock. Given the limitation on the speed of the motherboards, Intel boosted performance by making the CPU faster.

The existence of the two clocks explains the odd speeds of the processors. A Pentium running at 266MHz is actually running four times faster than the 66MHz motherboard, and a Pentium running at 350MHz is running approximately two-and-a-half times faster than the 133MHz motherboard. The CPU operates at the code processor frequency, which is quite fast. To communicate with the other components, it uses the lower, system bus frequency.

Also pay attention to the voltages at which the various CPUs operate. As the speed of the CPU increases, so does the temperature. The temperature increase is also proportional to the voltage applied to the CPU. The original Intel processors operated at 5 volts, but today's Pentium operate at 3.3 volts. The Pentium Pro processor operates at 1.5 volts. Some motherboard manufacturers let you specify the voltage of the CPU so that they can accommodate multiple CPU types. You'll be able to set the voltage through one or more jumpers on the motherboard, or through the BIOS Setup program.

Exercise

The CPU is inserted in either of two types of socket: a ZIF (Zero Insertion Force) socket, or one that looks like an expansion slot. PGA (Pin Grid Array) chips are usually Pentium CPUs and fit into ZIF sockets. Older CPUs, up to 486DX, come in PGA packages. A PGA chip has many pins arranged in four rows on every side. Pentium II and Pentium III CPUs come in SEC packages and are usually inserted like expansion boards, only they don't fit the usual expansion boards.

To Replace a PGA CPU

1. Turn off the PC and all peripherals, disconnect all cables, and remove the computer's cover (see Lab 5 for details).

2. Remove the existing CPU from the motherboard. To do so, lift the lever on one side of the CPU and gently remove the chip.

3. If needed, set the jumpers on the motherboard to reflect the type and speed of the new processor.

NOTE Even if it's outdated, place the old CPU chip in an antistatic bag and keep it. The old chip will probably come in handy in repairing an old computer with a CPU that has failed. These old CPUs are already hard to find.

---

4. Examine the PGA chip and you'll see that the arrangement of the pins is not symmetric. One of the corner pins is missing; this is the notch corner. The socket has the same pin arrangement, so use the notch corner to align the chip in its socket.

5. While the lever is lifted, insert the PGA chip in its socket, taking into consideration the chip's notch corner. Then lower the lever to lock the pins into place firmly.

6. Place the heat sink and fan on the CPU. The heat sink has two handles, one on each side, and you must latch on the matching handles located at the two sides of the CPU socket. The fan requires its own power and comes with a short power cord. You'll find a small power connector near the CPU on the motherboard. Older motherboards don't have a separate connector for the fan, so use one of the power cables that come out of the power supply.

7. Don't close the cover yet. Reinsert any of the boards you may have removed in order to reach the CPU or the jumpers on the motherboard. Connect the power plug, the monitor, and the keyboard, and turn the computer on. If it comes on, then the replacement operation was successful. If not, turn off the power and disconnect the cables. Make sure the chip is seated firmly on its socket and the jumpers are set correctly. Then close the computer and turn it on again.

8. If the computer doesn't recognize the speed of the new CPU, bring up the BIOS Setup program and make sure the settings are correct (see Lab 9 for details on the BIOS settings). If the system doesn't even come on, make sure the motherboard supports the CPU, the CPU is seated firmly in its socket, and you have set the jumpers on the motherboard for the speed of the CPU.

To Replace an SEC CPU

1. Turn off the PC and all peripherals, disconnect all cables, and remove the computer's cover (see Lab 5 for details).

2. Remove the existing CPU from the motherboard. To do so, locate the CPU package on the motherboard and remove it gently. There are no screws or latches holding it in place. If there's a fan on the package, write down how the fan's power cord is connected to the motherboard.

3. If needed, set the jumpers on the motherboard to reflect the type and speed of the new processor.

NOTE The old chip may come in handy in repairing an old computer with a CPU that has failed, so place it in an antistatic bag and keep it. These old CPUs are already hard to find.

---

4. Insert the new CPU package in the same slot. You won't be able to fit it into its slot the wrong way.

5. Now connect the fan's power cord to the motherboard. The connector should be near the CPU slot.

6. Don't close the cover yet. Reinsert any of the boards you may have removed in order to reach the CPU or the jumpers on the motherboard. Connect the power plug, the monitor, and the keyboard, and then turn the computer on. If it comes on, then the replacement operation was successful. If not, turn off the computer, disconnect the cables, and make sure the CPU is seated firmly in its slot and the jumpers are set correctly. Then close the computer and turn it on again.

7. If the computer doesn't recognize the speed of the new CPU, bring up the BIOS Setup program and make sure the settings are correct. See Lab 9 for details on system settings.

Lab 8

DATE _____ NAME _____

1. What's the type and speed of the processor currently in your computer?

_____

_____

_____

_____

2. What's the fastest CPU that can fit in your motherboard? Write down the settings of the jumpers on the motherboard that correspond to this CPU:

_____

_____

_____

_____

_____

3. Describe the following terms:

L1 and L2 cache

_____

_____

MMX

_____

_____

Overclocking

_____

_____

Pipelining

_____

_____

_____

4. What is an Overdrive chip?

_____

_____

_____

_____

5. Explain why increasing the clock rate doesn't necessarily make the CPU run faster.

_____

_____

_____

_____

Lab 9: CMOS Setup

Objectives for This Lab

Upon completion of this lab, you will be able to

1. Configure the BIOS on your computer.

2. Replace the CMOS battery.

Hardware & Software Requirements

Hardware: A working PC computer

Software: None for this lab

What to Read in the Book

Chapter 3, pages 160–61; Chapter 6, pages 374–79; Chapter 13, pages 556–59; Chapter 32, pages 1327–31, *The Complete PC Upgrade & Maintenance Guide*, Mark Minasi, Sybex

Introduction

The BIOS (basic input/output system) is the first program that's loaded when the computer is turned on. It's actually the BIOS that loads the operating system. The BIOS is a relatively short program, and its task is to enable the CPU to communicate with the peripherals, such as the keyboard, the monitor, and the hard disks. When the computer is turned on, the BIOS performs the Power On System Test (POST). During POST it detects the installed devices and configures them. To accomplish all these tasks, the BIOS needs to know about the various devices on the computer. Normally, the BIOS detects all the devices, but occasionally it may need some help. For example, you may have to tell it the current date, the boot order of the devices, and so on.

The BIOS program comes with the motherboard and must store the settings for that particular computer in nonvolatile memory (if not, you'd have to configure your computer every time you turn it on). The hard drive would be a good choice for storing these settings, but the information about the hard drive itself must also be stored along with the computer's settings. Since the BIOS needs information about the hard drives before it can access them (number of cylinders, sectors, and tracks), you can't store this information on a hard drive.

In the past, the solution has been to store the BIOS in a special read-only memory chip (ROM), which maintains its data even when the power is off (the data is "burned" into the chip). Older motherboards included the BIOS on a ROM chip. The limitation of this approach is that to change the BIOS, you must replace its ROM chip with another one, which you purchase from the BIOS manufacturer. You'll rarely need to replace a computer's BIOS outright, but manufacturers periodically release new versions, and occasionally a problem can be fixed by upgrading the BIOS to a newer version.

Modern motherboards store the BIOS in flash memory or in EEPROM (Electrically Erasable Programmable Read Only Memory), which can be updated under software control. (The newer flash memory technology is functionally equivalent to EEPROM; digital cameras use flash memory to store the images.) A computer's motherboard comes with a CD of utilities that include the software for downloading the BIOS upgrades. It is actually possible to upgrade the BIOS without reinstalling the operating system or the applications.

To find out whether a new version of your BIOS is available, visit the site of the BIOS manufacturer on the Web. Many computer manufacturers will purchase the BIOS and customize it. You should also check with the motherboard's manufacturer to find out the latest BIOS version you can install on your computer. Fortunately, the BIOS is fairly stable software and doesn't change frequently. Usually, there are no patches to be installed, either. In rare occasions you may have to update the BIOS, but in most cases when the BIOS becomes outdated, it's time for a new motherboard. There aren't that many BIOS manufacturers around, and it's easy to learn how to configure the most popular ones.

The Role of CMOS

Unlike the BIOS software, the settings of the BIOS—that is, your computer's parameters—can't be stored in ROM, because they need to be updated if hardware is added or replaced. Most motherboards use a special memory chip called CMOS (Complementary Metal-Oxide Semiconductor), for storing these settings. CMOS memory is powered by a battery so that it can maintain its data even when the main power is off. If you remove this battery, the CMOS memory's data will be lost.

The battery that powers the CMOS chip is a coin-type battery that is easy to find on the motherboard. The process of replacing the battery is outlined in this lab's exercise, "To Replace the CMOS Battery." When the battery is removed, the BIOS settings are lost and you must reconfigure the BIOS manually. Most CMOS chips will retain their contents long enough for you to replace the battery. In older motherboards, the BIOS will forget its settings as soon as you remove the battery. Newer motherboards provide a capacitor that enables the CMOS chip to retain its content for a while.

There are occasions when we actually want the computer to forget its settings (we may have forgotten the password and we want the computer to forget it, too, so that we can set a new one). In such a case, you must remove the battery and leave the computer turned off for a few hours, to make sure the CMOS chip has lost its contents.

On some systems the CMOS chip includes the memory and battery. These chips have a life of 10 years or so. If the computer is still operational after 10 years, you'll have to replace this chip, which is socketed on the motherboard.

Configuring the BIOS

As discussed in Lab 3, you should create a written backup of the BIOS settings in CMOS. This will help you restore those settings if the battery fails and must be replaced, or if the information is lost when you are taking apart your computer to replace or repair its components.

NOTE You can always restore the BIOS settings to their factory default values. These values may not reflect all the devices you have added to your computer, but it's a good starting point and your computer will be able to function.

To see and edit the BIOS settings, you'll use the BIOS Setup screen. Each BIOS has a different method of calling up this screen. When you turn on the computer, you'll see a message prompting you to press one or more keys in order to view the BIOS settings. The various BIOS versions use different keystrokes, such as F1 or F2 or the Del key, or sometimes a combination such as Control+Alt+S.

BIOS Setup is a text-based program, and you can't use the mouse to move around. To move from one item to the next, use the arrow keys. The current item is highlighted in reverse color. Most items have relatively few settings, and you aren't allowed to enter any text directly. Instead, press the Page Up and Page Down keys to scroll through the list of the valid values. Once you've reached the desired value for the selected item, you can move to the next item with the arrow keys.

The BIOS Setup utility lets you set up quite a few parameters, but here are the most important ones:

Date and Time The CMOS battery is also used to power a special chip that keeps track of time so that the computer displays the correct time even after it has been turned off.

Processor Speed Here you tell the BIOS about the CPU on the motherboard. You can even "overclock" the CPU a little to boost performance, but it's recommended that you don't. (An over-clocked system runs at a clock rate that's faster than the rate specified by the CPU's manufacturer. For more information on overclocking and its consequences, see the section "A Word on Over-clocking and Matching Clock Speeds" in Chapter 3 of *The Complete PC Upgrade & Maintenance Guide*.) If users complain about their computer being unstable, suspect overclocking. Open this screen to examine the settings of the CPU and bring it back to its normal clock rate.

Hard Drive Type This setting tells the BIOS about the hard drive(s) installed on your computer. Typically, the BIOS can auto-detect the type and capacity of the hard drives. Once detected, the parameters of the drives are stored in the CMOS chip and read from there when needed.

Serial/Parallel Ports   You can specify the type of the parallel port—ECP (enhanced capabilities port), EPP (enhanced parallel port), unidirectional/bidirectional—as well as the interrupts and I/O addresses of the serial port.

Exercise

To Replace the CMOS Battery

1. Turn off the computer and unplug all cables.

2. Start the BIOS Setup program and write down all the settings, as explained in Lab 3. If you know that certain values haven't been changed, there's no need to write them down.

3. Find the coin-type battery on the motherboard. Make sure it's held on the motherboard by a single clip.

NOTE   We have seen batteries wired to the motherboard—whether by design or soldered by a technician, we don't know. If the battery on your computer is wired to the motherboard, write down the polarity of the side that's soldered. Then cut the wire as close to the battery as possible.

---

4. Make a note of the correct polarity for the battery (it's usually printed on the battery's socket, but make a note of it anyway). Then remove the battery from the clip.

5. Insert the new battery under the clip, according to the correct polarity.

6. If the battery was soldered to a cable, solder the existing wire to the battery. Do it quickly, because the wire may get really hot and some of the heat will dissipate to the motherboard and the battery.

7. Close the case, connect the cables, and turn on the computer. The BIOS will load the default values. Follow the steps outlined in the following procedure to restore the appropriate values of the BIOS settings.

To Use the BIOS Setup Program

1. Start the computer and press the appropriate key combination to enter the BIOS Setup program. The options on the first screen you see will depend on your computer's BIOS. The options described here are from the AWARD BIOS, but other BIOS screens are similar.

The AWARD BIOS Setup program's main screen contains the following options, each of which leads to another screen. Open the related screens by selecting the option with the arrow keys and pressing Enter.

STANDARD CMOS SETUP	SUPERVISOR PASSWORD
BIOS FEATURES SETUP	USER PASSWORD
CHIPSET FEATURES SETUP	IDE HDD AUTODETECTION
POWER MANAGEMENT SETUP	SAVE & EXIT SETUP
PNP AND PCI SETUP	EXIT WITHOUT SAVING
LOAD BIOS DEFAULTS	
LOAD SETUP DEFAULTS	

2. Select the option STANDARD CMOS SETUP. Here you can set the date and time, as well as the types of disks installed on your system. You can also see the amount of memory detected by the BIOS, as well as the type of video adapter.

- If the amount of memory displayed isn't what you think it should be, it may be that the memory modules you have installed are of smaller capacity than you think, or the computer can't use the modules in one or more banks. One or more memory modules might be dead, but chances are you're using the wrong type of memory modules, or you haven't filled the memory banks in order (see Lab 13 for more information on upgrading the memory). Open the computer and check the placement of the memory modules on the motherboard.

- If you know the type of hard drive installed on the computer, you can enter the necessary information here. The various hard disk parameters are described in Labs 14 and 18. If you have no information about the hard drive(s), you can ask the BIOS to auto-detect the type of the hard drive.

Explore the options on the STANDARD CMOS SETUP and then press Escape to return to the main screen.

3. Select BIOS FEATURES SETUP to see the options related to the specific BIOS.

- The Virus Warnings option enables the BIOS's virus detection feature (this option is missing in older BIOS versions).

- The CPU Internal Cache Memory option lets you enable or disable the processor's cache memory. You can also set the external cache, if the BIOS supports it, by adding the extra memory on the motherboard and enabling the option External Cache Memory. The external cache memory can be 256KB or 512KB and, if the motherboard supports external cache, you should populate the cache memory.

- The Boot Sequence option lets you specify the order in which the BIOS will search the floppy and hard drives to find a bootable disk. Cycle through the values of this option and select the one that best suits your system.

- In the same screen, you may find options for setting the CPU speed. If the BIOS doesn't let you set the speed of the CPU, then you have a relatively old motherboard and the only way to change the speed of the CPU is by setting the appropriate jumpers on the motherboard. Depending on the BIOS and its version, you may find these options in the STANDARD CMOS SETUP screen. Change the CPU speed only after replacing the CPU. It can be set to Manual or Autodetect; the latter is the safest option. If you choose to set it manually, you'll see that the CPU speed is a combination of the bus's speed and the multiplier. Let's say you have a 66MHz bus and a 266MHz Pentium. The multiplier must be set to 4 so that the product of the bus speed times the multiplier will equal the CPU speed (4 × 66 is approximately 266).

NOTE You can increase either the CPU speed or the bus speed, but as a responsible technician, you shouldn't do either (and you should discourage users from doing so). Just keep in mind that these settings can help you "fix" a computer that's unstable.

- The DRAM Speed Selection option lets you set the speed of the memory, and the Wait State setting lets you specify the memory's wait states.

Press Escape to return to the main BIOS Setup screen.

4. Select the option IDE HDD AUTODETECTION. The BIOS will attempt to auto-detect the drives in the system. For every drive it finds, it will display the parameters. If it prompts you to select one of several options, press Enter. In general, the BIOS is very good at auto-detecting drives. If it can't detect your drive, return to the STANDARD CMOS SETUP screen and specify the drive's parameters manually. Write down the hard disk's characteristics just in case. You don't have to change the settings of the hard drives now. Just follow the steps to understand the procedure, but then reject all changes by not saving them, as explained in step 6.

5. The BIOS Setup program has other screens, as well. You can specify information such as a password (so that no one else can fiddle with the BIOS parameters on a computer), an option to load the factory defaults, and more. Go ahead and explore these options on your own.

6. If you have changed any of the BIOS parameters for this lab, select the option EXIT WITHOUT SAVING. The BIOS will prompt you to confirm this choice, and the computer will restart as usual. If you have messed up the BIOS settings, select LOAD DEFAULT VALUES from the main BIOS Setup screen to restore a set of values that will work. Then use your notes from Lab 3 to restore the original settings.

Lab 9

DATE _____ NAME _____

1. Write down the type and voltage of the CMOS battery on your motherboard.

   _____

   _____

2. Write down the physical characteristics of your hard drive(s) as reported by the BIOS Setup screen.

   _____

   _____

   _____

   _____

   _____

3. Explain the relation between the bus speed and processor speed. Where in the BIOS Setup program do you specify these properties? When should you overclock the CPU?

   _____

   _____

   _____

   _____

   _____

Lab 10: Replacing the Power Supply

Objectives for This Lab

Upon completion of this lab, you will be able to

1. Remove the computer's power supply.

2. Replace the power supply with a new one.

Hardware & Software Requirements

Hardware:

1. A working PC computer with Windows 95/98 installed

2. A Phillips screwdriver

3. An antistatic wrist strap

Software: None for this lab

What to Read in the Book

Chapter 9, pages 454–72, *The Complete PC Upgrade & Maintenance Guide,* Mark Minasi, Sybex

Introduction

There are two reasons you may need to replace a computer's power supply:

- The computer won't turn on because the power supply is broken.

This first scenario is quite clear-cut. If the power supply fails, it fails. And because of the very real danger of electrocution, you should never attempt to fix a broken power supply; just replace it.

TIP   If you do think your power supply is broken, before you replace it, make sure that the wall outlet is working and the computer's power cord is correctly plugged into both the computer and the wall outlet. You can also listen when you first turn on the PC, to hear if the fan that's attached to the power supply is working.

- The system is using wattage at or near the rating for your power supply, or you're planning a major upgrade.

Many of today's computers come with enough power to run the machine and all the attached peripheral devices just fine. But suppose you're beefing up the machine with, say, 256MB of RAM, a huge hard drive, and several other internal devices—all of which are going to draw on the power. In this case, you might well decide to take the precaution of upgrading to a 300-watt (or bigger) power supply. True enough, today's computers and their peripherals are far more energy efficient than in the past. Off-the-shelf 230-watt or even 180-watt models can service many more devices than was possible a few years ago. Nevertheless, if you pile on a CD-RW, a DVD, a second or third hard drive, and so on, you *can* exceed the power supply's capacity.

TIP   Don't be concerned about the cost of replacing a power supply. True, years ago they cost around $300 for a rock-bottom unit, but today they're around $25!

Evaluating your power requirements isn't quite so easy as simply replacing a broken power supply. The "watts capacity" specification isn't the same thing as "watts used." A 250-watt light bulb *does* use more than a 100-watt bulb—that's "watts used." But a 300-watt rating for a power supply means that it can convert *up to* 300 watts; if a system is currently requiring only 150 watts, that's all the wattage the power supply will convert. The important point is that you shouldn't push the power supply to convert so much energy that it is close to its maximum rating.

How do you know how much wattage your system is drawing? The easiest way to test it is to purchase a Power Meter from PARA Systems (see *The Complete PC Upgrade & Maintenance Guide,* Appendix A). This device resembles a power strip but has a meter that displays the amperes of current flowing into your system. Plug your system into the Power Meter, turn the system on, and check the Power Meter's gauge. You'll see a reading between 0.5 and 3.0. Multiply this reading by 58 to get the watts currently used by your system. If the watts-used value is close to the rating of your power supply, you'll want to buy a new power supply.

If you do decide to trade up, don't shop for just a *big* power supply. Try to get a big, *good* power supply. In *The Complete PC Upgrade & Maintenance Guide* , Mark Minasi recommends those manufactured by PC Power and Cooling (see the "What to Read in the Book" section just above).

Exercise

To Remove the Power Supply

1. Unplug the computer from the wall outlet, remove the power cord from the back of the computer, and remove the case.

2. On the back of the computer, remove the four screws that bolt the power supply to the computer.

3. Draw a diagram of the connections between your power supply unit and your hard drive(s), the tape, floppy and other drives, the fan, and the motherboard, and then unplug these connections. Note that except for motherboard connectors, which are larger, all the rest of the power connections look the same and are interchangeable. It does not matter which of them you attach to which hard drives and other devices—however, the length of a power wire can sometimes determine which devices it can reach.

TIP Remember, it is important to make that diagram. It'll be helpful for working with the On/Off switch and the motherboard, of course, but it's also useful because some peripherals are located farther from the power supply. Your diagram will show you what arrangement of wires works. Also make a drawing of the orientation of the power supply.

WARNING Some power supplies have two connections to the motherboard, and these connections are sometimes labeled P8 and P9. You must be careful to diagram these so that you do not reverse them when you install the new power supply. Otherwise, expect to see an interesting exhibition of smoldering as your motherboard self-destructs. The red wire is always closest to and facing the power supply. Usually, the connectors only go one way.

4. You'll see colored wires connecting the power supply to the computer's On/Off switch. Diagram these colored wires so you can later reattach them.

5. Remove the colored wires connecting the power supply to the computer's On/Off switch.

6. Remove the power supply.

To Install a New Power Supply

1. Using the four screws that you removed in step 2 of the procedure just above, attach the new power supply to the rear of the computer's case—in the same location and orientation as the previous power supply.

2. Now plug the large connector (or connectors) coming out of the power supply into the motherboard.

3. Using the diagram you drew when you removed the old power supply, attach the power supply to the On/Off switch.

4. Connect all the other devices (fan, drives, and so on). Recall that you can use any of the smaller (Molex and Berg) connectors with any of these devices. These connectors are interchangeable.

5. Finally, attach the computer's power cord to the power supply.

Lab 10

DATE _____ NAME _____

1. What should you check before installing a new power supply?

_____

_____

_____

_____

_____

2. Which of the power supply wires should be diagrammed?

_____

_____

_____

3. How do the connector(s) to the motherboard differ from the other power supply connectors?

_____

_____

_____

4. Does it matter which power supply connector you attach to a hard drive as opposed to a floppy drive?

_____

_____

Lab 11: Preventive Maintenance

Objectives for This Lab

Upon completion of this lab, you will be able to

1. Identify the major threats to a computer's good health.

2. Take steps that provide preventive maintenance.

Hardware & Software Requirements

Hardware:

1. A working PC computer

2. A surge protector and a power conditioner

3. A can of compressed air

4. A humidifier or an antistatic mat

5. Extra screws for the computer case

6. A lint-free cloth

7. Connector cleaner

8. An artist's eraser (the firm, white kind)

Software: None for this lab

What to Read in the Book

Chapter 4, *The Complete PC Upgrade & Maintenance Guide*, Mark Minasi, Sybex

Introduction

Just as it's usually better to fix medical problems before they become truly serious, preventive maintenance of PC hardware is almost always less difficult and less expensive than trying to cure a major problem later on.

What should you look for? What are the danger signs that a PC may experience trouble somewhere down the line? There are six enemies you should guard against:

- Heat
- Dust
- Magnetism
- Electromagnetism
- Power problems
- Water and other liquids

Some of these enemies are obvious. For example, don't leave a cup of coffee near the computer because it can easily be knocked over and spill onto key parts. You'll want to avoid zapping the computer (and yourself) by making sure you've discharged any static electricity you've built up, before touching any of the computer's chips (touch a metal desk to discharge yourself). To be completely safe, consider wearing an antistatic wrist protector, as well. Many experts recommend that a person be grounded properly before working on electrical components. And be sure you have a good UPS device to counteract power spikes.

But other enemies are sneaky. For example, few people realize that a little sunbeam can be a PC-killer. Keep a computer away from any window that casts direct sunlight. In addition, a kind of "sludge" can build up on computers used in nontraditional rooms such as kitchens. You may have noticed how cooking areas and workshop environments can, over time, accumulate a visible greasy coating on everything, including any nearby computers. Combine this with the dust in the air, and you get a sludge that can gum up the computer's works. The broader lesson here is that you need to evaluate every aspect of your computer's environment carefully in light of the hazards outlined in Chapter 4 of *The Complete PC Upgrade & Maintenance Guide*.

Exercise

To Provide a Safe Environment for a PC

1. Locate a power outlet that won't cause problems. For example, is the computer plugged into the same outlet as a space heater or coffeemaker? If so, find another outlet for the computer.

2. Does the PC share a circuit line with an air conditioner or other appliance that draws substantial power? If so, find another line for the PC.

3. Provide the computer with both a surge protector and a power conditioner.

4. Ensure that the room the computer is in doesn't become hotter than 110 °F or colder than 65 °F. You can permit it to get colder than 65 °F if you leave the computer turned on all the time—which is a very good idea.

TIP More and more, heat is a by-product of *overclocking* (or *pushing*), when people attempt to push their PC hardware for faster or otherwise better performance. This is usually done through tweaking the motherboard and CPU, and is increasingly being done with many video adapters. Overclocking involves adjusting the clock settings on the motherboard and CPU or on the video adapter. It can cause overheating as well as various hard-to-track-down random errors and device failures. Remember, your computer's designers had a particular speed in mind when they designed the machine's ventilation and provided such additional protection as heat sinks. If you find a machine that's been pushed, our advice is to restore it to its original clock speed.

5. Watch for dust build-up. Allowing a layer of dust to blanket computer chips is a sure way to overheat them. Use a can of compressed air (available at electronic supply stores) to periodically blow dust from the motherboard and other interior components of a computer.

6. Ensure that no vibration-causing peripherals (such as some of the old impact printers) share a table with the computer. This is bad for hard drives because the hard drive platters spin faster than you can imagine, and the read/write head rides on a tiny cushion of air only a hair above the platter. You don't want vibrations to cause the head to crash into the platter.

7. Guard against static electricity, which can weaken or kill chips. In the winter, when the humidity is low, take the precaution of touching a metal desk or some other object to discharge any static electricity from yourself. Other environmental solutions include using a humidifier, putting an antistatic mat under the computer, or installing static-free carpeting.

WARNING You can kill a computer chip with less than 35 volts of static electricity, but you can't *feel* a static charge in your body until it gets higher than 2,000 volts. Remember that you are always generating some amount of static electric charge. Err on the side of caution by always discharging yourself before getting your hands on the machine.

NOTE The foregoing preventive maintenance suggestions also apply to printers.

To Give a PC a Hands-on Health Checkup

1. Check the case screws. If any are missing, replace them. All those screws serve a purpose (see Lab 5).

2. Check whether the PC shares an outlet with big power users, such as portable heaters. If so, give the PC its own stable power source.

3. If the PC is near a window, make sure it never gets direct sunlight. If it does, put in drapes or move the computer away from the window.

4. Run the computer's diagnostic utility.

5. Run the Windows utility ScanDisk to see whether the hard drive needs defragmenting. Defragment it, if necessary.

6. Take off the cover and clean the edge connectors with a lint-free cloth. (Purchase some connector cleaner at an electronics store.) Alternatively, you can clean them with an artist's eraser (the firm, white kind), available in art supply stores.

7. Press the chips into their sockets (but don't push soldered chips).

TIP Computer chips creep out of their sockets over time, and this is another good reason to leave the computer's power turned on all the time. Turning the power on and off causes thermal changes that assist chips in climbing out of their sockets.

---

8. Blow out any dust with a can of compressed air before you replace the cover.

Lab 11

DATE _____ NAME _____

1. Describe three of the six main threats to a computer's good health.

_____

_____

_____

_____

_____

_____

_____

_____

2. List the steps you can take to guard against static electricity.

_____

_____

_____

_____

_____

_____

3. What should you check for at the wall plug where the computer gets its electricity?

_____

_____

_____

_____

_____

4. What should you look for if a computer sits near a window?

_____

_____

_____

Lab 12: Virus Protection

Objectives for This Lab

Upon completion of this lab, you will be able to

1. Understand how viruses work and how antivirus software fights them.

2. Install the Norton AntiVirus program and use it to scan a computer for viruses.

Hardware & Software Requirements

Hardware: A working computer with an Internet connection

Software: Norton AntiVirus 2000

What to Read in the Book

Chapter 15, *The Complete PC Upgrade & Maintenance Guide*, Mark Minasi, Sybex

Introduction

The best way to deal with viruses is to detect them before they're installed on your computer—in other words, prevent rather than heal.

Most people are scared of viruses and believe that when a virus infects their computer, all the data will be lost. Although some viruses have proven to be undeniably destructive, the truth is that the majority are relatively harmless—just annoying. What you should worry about is *how* the computer got infected and *why*. This helps you guide users about what files and messages they should avoid and what type of actions put their computers at risk.

If you're called to fix problems only, ask users to install antivirus software on all the machines you repair. Make sure users understand why the software must be updated frequently and show them how it's done. Best of all, explain to them how easy it is to contract a virus and that the only real protection is prevention. Antivirus software is a great tool, but you can't rely on the software alone.

If you're responsible for many computers in a corporation, install antivirus software on the computers in your care, and describe the early symptoms of a virus infection to the users. Have users report immediately to you anything viruslike noticed on their computer. The virus might already have spread to the entire network before it's detected on a particular machine, so check all the network's computers for viruses.

How Viruses Work

Viruses are small programs attached to COM or EXE files. You can copy a useful application to your computer and, without knowing it, copy the virus right along with the EXE file. You can also transfer a virus when you start your computer with an infected floppy disk. The virus is hidden in the floppy's boot record and copies itself to the hard drive. People no longer use floppies to start their computers, but they *do* use electronic mail. With the advent of the Internet and e-mail, there are more opportunities for viruses to spread (mainly as attachments).

Once a virus is copied to your computer, it usually remains silent for a while. Most viruses will first infect as many files as they can in your computer, and only then will the destructive part of the virus be activated. By infecting multiple files, a virus increases its chances of getting out of your computer and infecting another user's computer.

The destructive part of the virus is activated when an event takes place. For example, the virus may activate itself after it has infected a given number of files, or on Friday the 13th, or when you run a specific program, and so on. Some programmers simply want to demonstrate their ability to build a virus (especially one that will fool the antivirus software), but aren't bent on destroying the information on the user's disk. The "destructive" part of the virus may not be destructive at all, but this isn't something you can count on. Although most viruses are nothing more than annoying, you can't know that until it's too late. So better safe than sorry.

Viruses may reside in the following areas of the system:

- The MBR (Master Boot Record) or DBR (DOS Boot Record), so that they're loaded every time you start the computer. The MBR and DBR are crucial in booting a computer; for more information see Lab 2, "Starting the Computer."

- Any EXE or COM file (that is, any program). The specific program must be run in order to activate the virus. In other words, you can have an infected file on your drive, but if you don't execute it, the virus won't spread or harm your computer.

- A document created by an application that supports macros. A Word document, for example, may contain macros. When any of these macros is activated, the virus is also activated.

Deadly E-Mail

The latest virus-spreading technique is by e-mail. Once a computer gets infected, the virus prepares messages with copies of itself and sends them off to the addresses in the user's address book. The subject line is something like "An interesting program" or "Run this application." Recipients think the message came from a friend and they open it. When they attempt to execute the application, the virus installs itself and is ready to spread further (or do something harmful on the computer).

NOTE   Remember that an infected EXE that arrives as an attachment to a message is not a threat—as long you don't execute the application. Advise users never to open an executable attachment without some additional information from the sender. Users should at least verify that the listed sender is in fact the one who has sent the message *and* the attachment.

Who Loves You?

As of this writing, the latest vicious virus attack is the infamous ILOVEYOU virus (and its variations). It was extremely simple, written in a scripting language (VBScript), attached to a message with the subject "I LOVE YOU." The message contained a file with the extension ".TXT.VBS." Many people were fooled by the TXT extension, but the file's *real* extension was actually VBS. VBScript is a scripting language, similar to the batch language of DOS. Very few users would ever execute a BAT file sent to them via e-mail without examining its statements first. Apparently, however, many Windows users were unfamiliar with the VBS extension and executed the attached script without checking it first. The virus first transmitted copies of the original message to all the addresses listed in the user's Contacts folder, and then deleted some files in the user's System folder.

To be fair, it was more than the TXT extension that fooled people: The message with the attachment looked safe because it came from a friend. So it's important to educate users about the possibility that every message they receive nowadays is a potential intruder. Tell them never, *ever* to double-click an attachment unless they know and understand its extension. Extensions such as JPG and TIFF, for example, are harmless. Just make sure that these file types are associated with an image processing application. And users should make sure they've read the last part of the filename, as well. Any attachment with an odd or unusually long filename is reason for caution. That long filename may be hiding the extension of a destructive file.

How Antivirus Software Works

Modern antivirus software detects viruses by monitoring the activity of applications. If an application attempts to alter an EXE file, that application is considered suspect. An application does not usually modify its own EXE file, let alone another EXE file on the disk. Many popular antivirus programs create a *checksum* for each program file, as well as for the MBR and DBR. The checksum is a very long number based on the actual contents of a file and its length (the antivirus software actually scans the file's bytes to produce the checksum). If a virus attaches itself to the file, the new checksum won't match the original one, and the antivirus software will know that the file may have been infected.

Of course, there are hundreds of known viruses, which the antivirus software detects individually. Known viruses are easy to handle because someone has studied the virus, knows what it looks like, and has written code to detect and destroy it. Even if the antivirus software misses a virus, it won't be long before the virus acts on some other computers and is detected.

Antivirus software wouldn't be nearly as useful if it couldn't detect suspicious activity in the computer and stop new viruses from spreading. New viruses are reported daily, and it only takes 24 hours on average to write the code to handle it. When you buy an antivirus package, such as Norton AntiVirus and McAfee Antivirus, it's imperative that you update the software as frequently as possible. All you have to do is connect to the Internet and let the program download the updates. If you're attentive to the updates, you'll minimize the chances of your computers' being infected by a new and unknown virus.

The two most popular and most up-to-date antivirus tools today are

- Mc-Afee Virus-Scan (`www.mcafee.com/products/default.asp`)
- Norton AntiVirus 2000 (`www.symantec.com/nav/nav_9xnt/`)

Exercise

To Install and Use Antivirus Software

1. Install the Norton AntiVirus software on your computer. Download the trial version of Norton Antivirus 2000 from `www.symantec.com/nav/nav_9xnt/` and then run the installation program. You'll have to download a healthy number of megabytes to your computer, but if need be you can interrupt the download and continue at a later time without having to start over. (Symantec uses an intelligent component for downloading large files, which continues from where it left off the last time you were downloading.)

2. After the software is installed, you'll see the new Norton AntiVirus item in the Programs menu. Open this menu and select AntiVirus to run the program.

3. The main function of the antivirus software is to scan the hard disk and memory for viruses. You can check the boxes for all the hard drives, if you want. Before you scan the drives, however, take a look at the Options menu.

4. Click the Options button and you'll see another window with nine tabs. Here are descriptions of the most important tabs:

> **Scan** Here you specify where the software should look for viruses. Leave the options Memory, Master Boot Record, Boot Records, and Program Files checked. These are the areas where viruses reside.

> **Startup** On this tab you specify the areas to be scanned for viruses whenever the computer starts. Do not change the default settings here, either.

> **Auto-Protect** Here you specify how the virus protection works in the background. You want a virus to be detected the instant it enters your computer and removed on the spot. Norton AntiVirus can check a file for viruses the moment the file is created, copied, or executed. Remember that the virus can't spread unless you execute the EXE file that hides it.

5. After setting the options, return to the main window of AntiVirus and click the Scan button. The program will first scan the memory and the boot records. Then it will scan all the files in the specified drives for viruses. You may be surprised by the findings. The program will report all infected files as well as the virus that has infected them. It will also automatically clear all the viruses.

6. Another command in the Tools menu is Inoculation. Select this command and you'll be prompted to specify the item you want to inoculate. When you inoculate a file or the boot record, Norton AntiVirus creates a unique signature for it. On subsequent scans, the program calculates the file's signature again and compares it to the stored value. If the two values agree, the file is clean. If they don't agree, this is an indication that the file could be infected.

TIP Some EXE files, however, alter themselves. If certain EXE files in your network modify themselves frequently, you can uninoculate them with the Uninoculate command. The software will notify you the moment an inoculated file's signature changes. If an EXE file is being modified when it's executed, you should probably uninoculate it.

---

7. The next step is to connect to the Internet and download all the software's updates. Click the Live Update button on the main AntiVirus window.

NOTE The Live Update feature is disabled in the demo version—that's how Symantec gets you to buy the AntiVirus software. Even if you spend only $50 a year for software, spending it on anti-virus software is a wise investment. Buy the software, register it immediately, and update as frequently as you can.

8. One of the programs that come with Norton Antivirus is the Rescue Disk program. It creates a set of five floppies, which you can use to start the computer if a virus damages the MBR. First scan your computer for viruses (steps 2 through 5) and, if it's clean, create the Rescue Disks immediately.

   Hopefully, you'll never have to use the Rescue Disks, but if a malicious virus finds its way to your computer, you'll be glad you created them. We suggest keeping a second set of Rescue Disks on hand for every PC in the organization. The Rescue Disks created for a specific PC can't be used on another machine.

Lab 12

DATE _____ NAME _____

1. How do viruses work?

_____

_____

_____

_____

2. What type of activity does the antivirus software monitor in order to detect viruslike activities?

_____

_____

_____

_____

3. How do viruses infect computers?

_____

_____

_____

_____

4. Is it enough to scan your computer for viruses every time you turn it on, or not? Explain why.

_____

_____

_____

_____

Lab 13: Adding Memory

Objectives for This Lab

Upon completion of this lab you will be able to

1. Add memory to your computer.

2. Replace existing memory modules.

Hardware & Software Requirements

Hardware:

1. A working PC computer

2. An antistatic wrist strap

3. A Phillips screwdriver

4. SIMM or DIMM memory modules

Software: None for this lab

What to Read in the Book

Chapter 3, pages 138–74; and Chapter 8, *The Complete PC Upgrade & Maintenance Guide*, Mark Minasi, Sybex

Introduction

After the CPU, memory is the second most important part of your computer, and the amount of memory installed can make a real difference in performance, especially if you're running Windows. Windows can use up lots of memory—more than users can afford. So Windows employs a segment of the hard drive as memory. The hard drive isn't nearly as fast as RAM, but it's much cheaper. The more memory in your computer, the more programs you can have in memory, and the faster you can switch among them. If Windows has to copy part of the memory onto the hard disk to make room for another application, performance degrades noticeably.

Memory chips are classified according to their type and packaging. The most common type of memory used in older 486 and Pentium computers is Dynamic RAM (DRAM). Another popular type of memory is EDRAM (Enhanced Dynamic RAM). Most new computers come with another type of RAM, Synchronous DRAM (SDRAM), which is faster than EDRAM. Read the motherboard's manual to find out the type of memory you can install.

Another factor to consider is the physical configuration of the memory. Most of the older computers out there (the 486 and older Pentium machines) use a package type known as SIMM (Single Inline Memory Module). Newer designs use DIMM (Double Inline Memory Module). Both are small circuit boards populated with memory chips. SIMMs come in either 30-pin or 72-pin format. DIMMs come in 168-pin format and they install in a different type of socket.

NOTE SIMMs are installed in pairs. Computers that require SIMMs have clearly marked banks (Bank 0, Bank 1, and so on), and you must fill them in order, starting with the lowest-numbered bank. You can't fill Bank 2 without filling Banks 0 and 1. Each bank consists of two sockets, and you must insert modules of the same capacity in both sockets. DIMMs are longer than SIMMs and are not paired, but they fill the available banks in order. Some motherboard manufacturers don't label the memory banks as Bank 0, Bank 1, and so on. If you're not certain as to which is the first bank, consult the motherboard's documentation. A motherboard whose memory banks are labeled as DIMM1, DIMM2, and so on, may require that you populate the bank DIMM4 first.

Unfortunately, you can't keep adding memory to your computer. Eventually, you will run out of sockets, and you may have to remove some of the existing modules to replace them with higher-capacity ones. Do not fill the sockets with 2MB or 4MB modules just because they're cheaper than 8MB or 16MB modules. You'll just fill up all the sockets with low-capacity modules and then will have to remove some of the existing modules.

TIP It's rather unlikely that you will ever install memory in blocks smaller than 32MB, but the number of memory banks and the capacity of the modules in each bank is a major consideration when buying a new computer. Go for the highest-capacity modules so that you'll have room to expand. 128MB of RAM in 4 modules of 32MB is a little less expensive than 2 modules of 64MB each, but far more expensive when it comes to upgrading. You should also consider the amount of memory your motherboard can see. Don't go out and buy the highest-capacity modules until you make sure your motherboard can accommodate them.

If the computer doesn't work with the new memory, you have probably used the wrong type of memory. Check the motherboard's manual to find out the exact specifications of the memory modules and, if needed, call the motherboard's manufacturer to get more information. If you're not using a generic computer, the memory supplier will also be able to help you. Just ask for memory to fit the specific make and model of your machine.

Memory speed is another consideration. You should consult your motherboard's manual to find out the memory speed it supports, and purchase the appropriate modules. If the memory modules you're using are too fast for the bus, then you'll have to increase the number of *wait states* in the BIOS setup. The typical access time for DRAM memory is between 50 and 100 nanoseconds. This speed roughly matches, at best, a processor running at 100MHz. Since there's no DRAM that matches the fastest processors, motherboard designers make the CPU wait for the data to arrive from the memory by increasing the memory's wait states.

Mixing memory modules of different speeds is also not a good idea. When you can't find modules of the exact same speed as the existing ones, you can try and use memory with a similar speed. But if the computer refuses to see the faster memory (it may not even see any memory at all), you must adjust the wait states setting in the BIOS. Increase the number of wait states (which are expressed in clock cycles) and see if it helps.

Exercise

If you're replacing the memory on a 486 computer, each bank has a single SIMM. Starting with the Pentium motherboards, each memory bank consists of two SIMM modules. DIMM modules can be used with Pentium motherboards only, and they don't appear in pairs.

Some boards, especially the ones with Pentium MMX processors, can accept both SIMM and DIMM modules. The memory modules in these boards must be filled in a specific order; consult the motherboard's documentation for the details.

To Remove Existing SIMM Modules

If all the memory slots are taken, you may have to remove some of the existing, low-capacity modules and replace them with high-capacity ones. To remove SIMM modules, start with the highest-numbered banks.

1. Turn off the computer and disconnect all power cables. Make sure you're wearing an antistatic wrist band before you touch the memory modules.

2. Open the computer and locate the highest-numbered banks that are already filled.

3. Release the latches that hold the SIMM modules in place. These latches are located on either side of the module. Press them gently outward to release the module.

WARNING   Do not apply excessive force on the latches. If you break a latch in a memory slot, this slot will become unusable. Break two latches and you'll buy a new motherboard.

4. Then pull the module forward to disengage it from the socket, and lift it.

5. Repeat the same process for the other module in the same bank.

6. Repeat the preceding three steps for all the banks you want to empty.

7. If you don't want to add memory modules at this time, close the computer and turn it on.

To Insert New SIMM Modules

1. Insert the module into the lowest-numbered bank that's free. Hold the module at a slight angle, and look for a notch; align it with the notch on the socket. You won't be able to insert the module backwards; if you do, you've probably broken the socket.

2. Push the module into the socket until it latches. Don't push hard; if the module doesn't latch easily, you're probably trying to insert it the wrong way.

3. Plug in all the cables and turn the computer on. Don't close the cover yet.

4. If the computer sees the new memory, turn off the computer, close the case, and turn it on again. If the new memory isn't recognized, repeat the insertion process and make sure the modules are seated firmly. If you repeat the process several times and the computer refuses to see the memory, exchange the memory modules for new ones.

To Remove Existing DIMM Modules

1. To remove a DIMM module, release the latches that hold it in place by pressing them down toward the sides of the module.

2. After the module has been disengaged from its socket, pull it gently upward to remove it from its socket.

3. Repeat steps 1 and 2 for all the DIMM modules you want to remove from the motherboard.

4. If you don't want to add memory modules at this time, close the computer and turn it on.

To Insert New DIMM Modules

1. DIMM modules don't have a notch to help you align them in their sockets. However, their contacts are grouped, and each group consists of a different number of contacts. Match the groups of contacts in the module to the groups of contacts in the socket.

2. The two latches on either side of the module must be open. If not, press them down to open them.

3. After you have inserted the module initially in the socket, press it gently downward and it will latch easily. Do not force it into place.

4. Now push the two latches up to lock the module in place.

5. Turn the computer on. If it sees the additional memory, turn the computer off and close the case. If the memory isn't recognized, turn the computer off, reseat the modules, and try again. If you repeat the process several times and the computer refuses to see the memory, exchange the memory modules for new ones—but not before you verify once again that the motherboard supports the total amount of memory you're trying to install.

Lab 13

DATE _____ NAME _____

1. What's the difference between static and dynamic RAM?

_____

_____

_____

_____

2. What's the function of the cache memory on the CPU?

_____

_____

_____

_____

_____

3. A computer has two memory banks and one of them contains 4MB modules. You're asked to upgrade the memory to 32MB or a little more. What modules would you use and why?

_____

_____

_____

_____

4. Explain why it's better to spend money on more memory rather than faster and more expensive memory.

_____

_____

_____

Lab 14: The Hard Drive

Objectives for This Lab

Upon completion of this lab, you will be able to

1. Understand the physical and logical organization of a computer hard disk.

2. Use the Disk Editor utility to explore the structure of a floppy disk.

Hardware & Software Requirements

Hardware:

1. A working PC computer

2. A blank floppy diskette

3. A connection to the Internet (optional)

Software: Disk Editor (you can download it from the Internet)

What to Read in the Book

Chapter 10 and Chapter 14, *The Complete PC Upgrade & Maintenance Guide,* Mark Minasi, Sybex

Introduction

Nearly every part or device in the computer case is a "black box." You connect it to the motherboard, and once the motherboard sees it you're done. How the device works is not your problem. All you care is that it works; when it doesn't, you simply replace it.

Hard drives are different. You need a basic understanding of their physical and logical structure so that you can maintain them in good shape and fix them when they develop minor defects.

The Drive's Physical Characteristics

Physically, hard disks are organized by *tracks*, *cylinders*, and *sectors*:

Tracks Tracks are concentric circular areas of the disk. As such, the length of a track is the circumference of the disk. Of course, tracks closer to the disk's center have a smaller circumference.

Hard drives store the same amount of information on every track, so the inner tracks are recorded more densely than the outer tracks.

Cylinders   Hard drives have multiple platters and a separate read/write head for each platter. All the heads are attached to a bracket, which is the *actuator arm*. This means that when one head is over a specific track in one platter, all other heads are over the same track in their corresponding platters. The set of all tracks with the same position on all platters is a cylinder. As you can see in Figure 14.1, the cylinder is not a physical entity of the drive. It's a *virtual* cylinder made up of many tracks.

To read data as fast as possible, the hard drive should keep all read/write heads busy. This is possible if consecutive segments of the same file are stored in the tracks of the same cylinder. The hard drive, therefore, reads all the tracks of the same cylinder at once, even if some of them are going to be ignored. This is why many people do not distinguish between the terms *cylinders* and *tracks*. For read/write operations, the two terms are the same.

F I G U R E   14.1   Tracks and cylinders on a disk

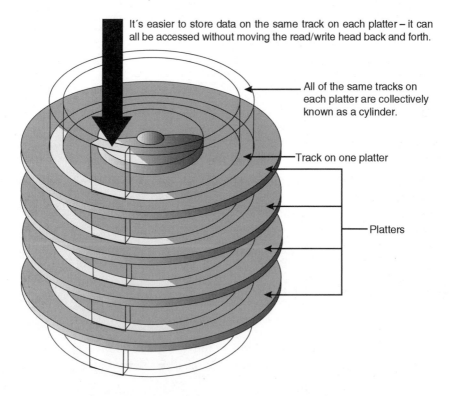

It's easier to store data on the same track on each platter – it can all be accessed without moving the read/write head back and forth.

All of the same tracks on each platter are collectively known as a cylinder.

Track on one platter

Platters

Sectors   Each platter is also divided into wedges, like a pie. As a result, the tracks are also divided into smaller pieces, which are called sectors. The sector is the smallest addressable part of the disk. Typically, a sector contains 512 bytes of data.

So let's do some calculations. Suppose a hard drive has 16,383 tracks, 16 read/write heads, and 63 sectors per track. The capacity of this disk is 8.4GB (16,383 tracks × 16 heads × 63 sectors/track × 512 bytes/head = 8,455,200,768 bytes, which is approximately 8GB). As you may have noticed, 16,383 is not a power of 2 (16,384 is the next power of 2) and neither is 63 (64 is). The disk actually has 16,384 tracks and 64 sectors per track, but not all of them can be used for storing data. Some tracks and some sectors are used as guides by the servomechanism that controls the movement of the hard drive's heads.

The Drive's Structure

The physical characteristics of the drive comprise all the information the BIOS needs to access the disk. The BIOS, however, isn't responsible for storing files to a drive or reading data from a drive. That is the job of the operating system. Different operating systems organize hard drives differently. DOS groups sectors into clusters. A cluster is the minimum space that can be allocated to a file. Even if a file contains a single byte, it will occupy an entire cluster on the disk. Since the cluster is made up of sectors and each sector stores 512 bytes, DOS may waste a kilobyte or more to store this file.

This seems like a terrible waste—and it is. The justification is that DOS must maintain a list of cluster addresses—the File Allocation Table (FAT), a large table that stores the addresses of all the clusters belonging to a file. The smaller the cluster size, the larger the tables that hold the addresses. This organization of the disk is dictated by the fact that the BIOS doesn't spend its time searching for contiguous free clusters to store the file. Rather, it uses free clusters as it finds them and then writes the addresses of these clusters to the FAT. This process speeds up the storing of a file, but it fragments the disk. In Lab 20, you'll learn how to defragment a hard drive and rearrange the disparate clusters of a file into contiguous ones.

Each cluster has its own entry in the FAT. The entry can be 0 (if the cluster is free); EOF (a value from hex FFF8 to FFFF, indicating that it's the last sector of a file); Bad (the hex value FFF7, indicating that the cluster is unusable); or a nonzero cluster address, which is the address of the next cluster in the file.

A new FAT structure was introduced with Windows 95: the VFAT, which supports long filenames. Windows 98 can use either FAT16 (which is equivalent to VFAT), or FAT32 (which supports very large disks and wastes less space than FAT16).

The Drive's Logical Structure

A physical drive can be partitioned into two or more logical drives. The physical drive is the one seen by the BIOS, whereas the logical drives are the ones seen by the operating systems. If you install different operating systems on the two drives, neither OS will be able to see the other's area. As you will see in Lab 17, you can partition a drive into a primary DOS partition and a non-DOS partition. Then you can install the Linux operating system (for example) on the non-DOS partition. The first sector in each partition must be the operating system's boot record.

Most PC users partition their drives either for organizational purposes or because they want to minimize the wasted space by reducing the cluster size. One of the partitions contains a DOS boot record; the others don't.

Exercise

To Calculate Floppy and Hard Drive Parameters

1. A 3.5" floppy disk has a capacity of 1.44MB and a cluster size of 512 bytes. You know that the floppy drive has two heads, because it's two-sided. With this information, you can calculate the total number of sectors on a floppy as follows:

   ```
   1,457,664 / 512 = 2847 sectors
   ```

   (The exact size of a 1.44MB floppy in bytes is 1,457,664, which you can verify with the CHKDSK A: command at the DOS prompt). DOS refers to sectors as *allocation units*. That's why, when you check the disk with the CHKDSK command, it reports 2847 allocation units.

2. The floppy has 80 tracks (cylinders) per side, so there are 18 sectors per track:

   ```
   2847 / (2 × 80) = 18 sectors
   ```

3. Start the BIOS Setup program and examine the parameters of the hard drive(s) on your system. Then repeat the calculations of steps 1 and 2 for the hard drive(s).

To Explore the FAT and Directory Structures

In this next procedure you'll actually "see" the structure of a floppy disk. We'll use a shareware application to look at the contents of the FAT, which only works with FAT16. As far we know, there are no tools for viewing FAT 32 and editing it directly—at least, these utilities are no longer popular. This exercise is meant to demonstrate how the FAT is organized, and it's not a blueprint for recovering accidentally deleted files by editing the FAT.

All utilities that manipulate binary files use hexadecimal notation. To convert between hex and decimal numbers, use the Windows Calculator in Scientific mode. If you're not familiar with hexadecimal notation, see Appendix B of *The Complete PC Upgrade & Maintenance Guide*.

1. To download the Disk Editor utility, enter the URL

   ```
   http://hotfiles.zdnet.com/cgi-bin/texis/swlib/hotfiles/
   info.html?fcode=000Q5F
   ```

in your browser's Address box, and when you see the utility's download page, click the Download Now button. The Disk Editor utility comes in a small Zip file, which you can unzip into a new directory on your hard disk and use to examine your drives.

WARNING   Although Disk Editor allows you to edit the disk directly, do *not* use it for that purpose. You may render the hard drive unusable by changing even a single byte of the DOS Boot Record. Use the Disk Editor utility simply to explore how DOS organizes the floppy drive, and *not* to edit any files. To experiment with Disk Editor, use a floppy. After you're comfortable with Disk Editor's interface and have developed an understanding of the organization of your drives, only then consider using it to edit the contents of your hard drives directly. Even so, we suggest you avoid editing the FAT to recover an accidentally deleted file. A single mistake, and an entire subdirectory (or the entire drive) may become unusable.

2. The Disk Editor utility, file DE.EXE, is a DOS program, which you must run from the DOS prompt. Open a DOS Prompt window, switch to the directory that contains the Disk Editor utility, insert a floppy containing a few files into drive A, and issue the following command:

   DE A:

3. Disk Editor will display the beginning of the first sector on the disk. Press F4 repeatedly to scroll through successive sectors on the disk, until you see the disk's directory (a list of filenames followed by a bunch of numbers). Figure 14.2, for example, shows the FAT of a bootable hard drive.

FIGURE 14.2   Viewing a disk's directory with Disk Editor

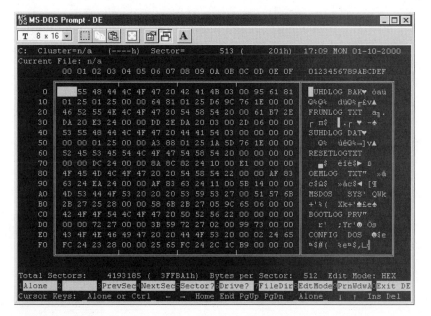

4. Notice that each filename is stored in 11 consecutive bytes (assuming the floppy doesn't contain any files with long names). Sixteen bytes after the name of each file, you'll find the two bytes with the address of the sector, where the file's contents are written; for example, F9 08. The address of the sector in hex is 08F9, which is 2297 in decimal notation.

5. Press F4 until you reach sector 2297, and you'll see the first characters in the file. To get there faster, press F5, enter **2297** as the cluster number, and when Disk Editor takes you there, press F4 a few more times to get to the desired sector.

6. Now return to the directory listing and press F5. When you're prompted for the cluster number, enter 0.

7. When you get to the first cluster, press F4 a few times. The two bytes following the address of the file's first cluster are the file's size. The values 70 9B, for example, are the hex value 9B70, which corresponds to the decimal value 39,792.

8. Continue using the Disk Editor utility to explore the structure of the FAT. For complete information about the structure of the FAT and the directory, refer to the section "The FAT and the Directory" in *The Complete PC Upgrade & Maintenance Guide*, page 643.

Lab 14

DATE _____ NAME _____

1. Draw a diagram of a hard disk, showing the platters, tracks, and sectors. How do we calculate the total capacity of a disk from its parameters?

_____

_____

_____

_____

2. Describe the role of the FAT.

_____

_____

_____

3. How many FAT entries will correspond to a file of 38,506 bytes on your hard drive?

_____

_____

Lab 15: Installing a Hard Drive

Objectives for This Lab

Upon completion of this lab, you will be able to

1. Install a new hard drive.

2. Replace an existing hard drive.

Hardware & Software Requirements

Hardware:

1. A working PC computer

2. A new hard drive (optional)

3. An antistatic wrist strap

4. A Phillips screwdriver and a flat screwdriver

5. Pliers to change jumper settings

Software: None for this lab

What to Read in the Book

Chapter 11, pages 544–46, *The Complete PC Upgrade & Maintenance Guide*, Mark Minasi, Sybex

Introduction

Installing a hard drive is the most common type of upgrade or repair you will perform on a computer. Most computers will develop a hard drive failure at some point. This lab shows you how to remove a hard drive from a computer and how to replace it with a new drive. Many computers eventually need a second hard drive added. Adding a second drive is a bit more complicated, and that process is described in Lab 18.

If the computer's drive (or one of its drives) malfunctions before failing and you suspect you must replace it, you should add a new drive while the old one is still functional. This allows you to copy your data files directly from the old disk to the new. You should also install the operating system to the new drive, so that when the old drive dies you'll still have a functional computer.

You'll encounter two types of hard drives: IDE (Integrated Device Electronics) and EIDE (Enhanced IDE). IDE drives are older and, most likely, will have to be replaced with an EIDE drive. As far as connectors go, the two hard drive types are identical. They both connect to the motherboard through a 40-pin flat ribbon cable, and to the power supply with a four-wire power cable. SCSI drives are different and they're discussed in Lab 23.

WARNING   Before you replace an existing hard drive, or even add a second hard drive, be sure to back up all your data. If you're replacing an existing drive because you suspect it's starting to fail (in other words, you're getting disk read or write errors), don't use your regular backup medium. You may corrupt a perfectly good backup.

Examine the hard drive (Figure 15.1) and you'll see two connectors and a few jumpers on the back. The first connector is a 40-pin connector, where the drive's data cable is attached. This is a ribbon cable, and its other end is connected to the drive control, which is usually on the motherboard (there are two hard drive controllers on the motherboard).

F I G U R E   15.1   Typical IDE/EIDE hard disk connections

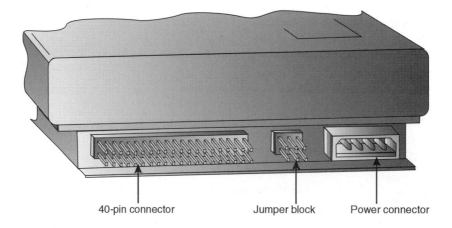

40-pin connector   Jumper block   Power connector

The second connector is a power connector, into which you must fit a Molex plug coming from the power supply. The jumpers on the back of the hard drive let you specify whether the drive will be the master or slave drive if you connect two hard drives on the same IDE connector on the motherboard. (We'll come back to the topic of multiple hard drives in Lab 18.) By default, all new drives come configured as master drives; nevertheless, make sure that the jumpers on the back of the hard drive are set for master configuration.

There are two types of data cables: those with a single hard drive connector and those with two hard drive connectors. The cables with two connectors are used to connect two drives to the same connector on the motherboard. If you want to connect two drives to the same cable, you'll need the data cable with the two connectors. Notice that the section of the cable between the two connectors is not twisted, as it is with the floppy drive's data cable.

TIP Before installing additional drives to your computer, make sure the power supply is adequate. Most power supplies are rated at 200 watts, which is plenty for the motherboard and two hard drives. If your computer's power supply is rated at less than 200 watts, or you're about to add a third drive, you should first install a 250-watt power supply.

DOS Issues

DOS can't see drives larger than 2.1GB and machines still exist out there that use DOS. The simplest method to make use of a large drive with DOS is to partition it into several smaller logical drives. Most of the drive won't be used anyway, because the hard drive requirements of typical DOS application don't come near the requirements of Windows applications. If you really need a very large drive for your DOS applications, consider installing Windows, use FAT32 for your drives, and then run the DOS applications in DOS windows.

Because of the DOS limitation on the drive size, some older motherboards may not see the drive's full capacity. The solution here is to replace the motherboard, but it doesn't make a lot of sense to upgrade the motherboard of a computer that will be used with DOS. If you run into this situation, you have two choices. You can let the drive function as the drive size perceived by the BIOS (if the BIOS sees the drive at all), regardless of the drive's actual (larger) size. Or you can buy a third-party disk management program; several good ones on the market today overcome the BIOS drive-size limitation. Check out Disk Manager DiskGo! (by OnTrack), Drive Up (by FWB Software), and EZ Drive (by MicroHouse). These programs work by telling the BIOS that the drive is a smaller size, and then using a driver loaded at startup to amend that data so that the full size of the drive can be recognized by the operating system when it loads.

Exercise

To Remove an Existing Hard Drive

Eventually, you will have to replace a dead hard drive, or replace a working hard drive that's too small and/or too slow. In this lab, you'll learn how to replace an IDE/EIDE drive. For the purposes of this lab, you'll remove and then reinstall the primary drive of your computer. (If you have a spare hard drive in the lab, use it to replace the existing one. When you're done, you must pull the replacement drive back out again and put the original one back in.)

1. Turn off the computer, disconnect all cables, and open the case.

2. Locate the drive you want to remove. There may be multiple hard drives in the computer case and their connectors are quite similar. Be sure you're removing the correct drive.

3. Notice how the ribbon cable is connected to the drive. The ribbon cable's red wire corresponds to pin 1 on the drive's connector. Write down the orientation of this pin, because not all connectors are properly labeled and data cables can be inserted the wrong way.

4. Remove the drive's data cable and power cable from the drive. Do not pull on the ribbon cable itself, because you may pull it out of its connector. Instead, try to pry the cable's connector out of the drive's connector. Use a flat screwdriver to loosen the cable's connector, if you have to. If you do take the cable apart, unplug the cable's connector from the drive and *don't* try to fix the cable. Find a spare, or buy a new one; they're quite inexpensive.

   If the arrangement of the cables on the drives makes it difficult to remove them while the drive is in place, move ahead to step 5 and then come back and unplug the data cables.

5. Release the screws that hold the existing drive on the bay and attempt to slide the drive out of its bay. There are four screws, two on either side of the drive.

6. Some older drives can be pulled out from the front of the computer case. With most drives, you'll have to slide the drive inside the case, and there may not be enough room to pull the drive entirely out of the bay. You may have to remove additional cables (most often the floppy cables). Remove all the cables that are in the way, but not before you label them and write down how they're connected. These cables must be plugged back in.

7. Once the drive is out of the bay, handle it carefully. Most IDE/EIDE drives are not totally enclosed in a metal case, and you can see the electronics at the bottom. Do not touch the electronics while handling the drive.

8. Information about the drive's physical characteristics should be printed on the drive itself; write this all down. You'll also see a set of jumpers at the back of the drive. These jumpers are used to configure a drive as master or slave. In this exercise you won't change these jumpers. Just examine their settings and verify the drive's documentation.

9. If there are additional hard drives in the computer, take note of how they're connected to the data cable(s) and how each data cable is connected to the motherboard.

To Add a Hard Drive

In this exercise, you're going to reinsert the drive you just removed. If you're actually going to replace the drive you just removed, start with step 2.

NOTE This is the procedure you'll follow to replace an existing hard drive. To add a second hard drive, follow the procedure shown in Lab 18.

1. If the computer you're working with has two (or more) hard drives, take a look at the jumpers next to the data cable connector on the back of the drive. The jumpers on the new drive should be configured exactly like the ones on the drive you're replacing.

2. If the drive is larger than 2GB there's a chance that an older BIOS won't see the drive. In this case you should probably replace the BIOS (if a newer version is available and if the BIOS is upgradeable), or the motherboard itself.

3. Connect the data cable and power cable to the new hard drive. Make sure the data cable is oriented properly. The power cable can't fit the wrong way.

4. Now insert the new drive in its bay. This step may be quite challenging if there's not enough space in the case. A common trick is to partially insert the drive into the bay, plug in the cables, and then push the drive into place.

5. The new drive is held into place by four screws, two on each side. Be sure to use all four screws. Some drives are too small for the computer's bay. These drives usually come with a bracket that you must screw on the drive; then you screw the bracket on the bay. For placement of the bracket, see the diagram that comes with the drive.

6. Close the computer's case, connect all the cables, and power up the computer. Even if it's a new drive, the BIOS should recognize it. If not, format the drive with the FORMAT command, which is described in Lab 16. If you want to create partitions, use the FDISK utility, which is described in Lab 17. Notice that if you attempt to FDISK a hard drive larger than 2GB, FDISK will ask you whether you want to install support for large drives. If you choose Yes, FDISK will convert the drive to FAT32. Select FAT32 unless the computer uses DOS. DOS can't see FAT32 drives, so you'll have to partition the drive into logical drives that don't exceed 2GB each. The DOS version that ships with Windows 95/98 supports FAT32 and can see large drives.

7. If you're replacing an existing hard drive, you'll have to install the operating system and all applications from scratch (you will have to do this if the old drive is dead). If you're adding a second drive (see Lab 18), you'll probably keep the old drive as the boot drive and use the second one to install applications and save data files. If the new drive is considerably faster than the old one, you should make it the boot drive and install the operating system on it.

Lab 15

DATE _____ NAME _____

1. Describe how the data cable is connected to the hard drive(s) of your computer.

_____

_____

_____

_____

2. Write the physical characteristics of the drive(s) in your computer. You'll have to slide each drive out of its bay (at least partially) to be able to read this information.

_____

_____

_____

_____

_____

3. What's the rating of the power supply? Did you have to replace it?

_____

_____

_____

_____

_____

Lab 16: Formatting

Objectives for This Lab

Upon completion of this lab, you will be able to

1. Format a disk from either DOS or Windows.

2. Create an emergency boot diskette.

Hardware & Software Requirements

Hardware:

1. A working PC computer with Windows 95/98

2. One or two floppy diskettes

Software: None for this lab

What to Read in the Book

Chapter 13, pages 629–31; Chapter 16, pages 713–15, *The Complete PC Upgrade & Maintenance Guide,* Mark Minasi, Sybex

Introduction

When you install a new hard drive, you may have to format it, but if you install an operating system on that drive, the installation process will format it for you.

Most hard drives come already formatted, as do diskettes. This wasn't always the case, but the time-consuming job of laying down tracks and sectors for today's multigigabyte hard drives is best left to the factory. In fact, if you had to do a low-level format for a large drive, you'd be able to do little else with that computer for quite some time.

There are two kinds of formatting: low-level and high-level. *Low-level formatting* divides the hard drive into zones called *tracks* and *sectors* that are used by the operating system to store files in an organized way.

High-level formatting doesn't mark off tracks and sectors; they are assumed to exist on the disk already. Rather, it merely replaces some of the organizational information on the drive: the file allocation table (FAT), the boot sector, and the root directory.

- The FAT is the disk's map of the files stored on that disk. This map allows the operating system (OS) to retrieve or replace a file because each file's clusters are specified in the FAT. Think of it as a catalog of the contents of the disk.

- The boot sector is a launching pad for the OS. It specifies the location of the FAT, so when the OS starts up, it knows where to find the diagram of the boot disk's contents. If the FAT is damaged, the computer will have problems knowing what's on the disk. As a safety measure, two copies of the FAT are stored on each disk.

- The root directory is the fundamental disk directory, from which any other directories must branch. The root directory cannot be deleted.

Although you generally don't need to do a low-level format to a disk, you will sometimes want to do a high-level format. There are several reasons to do a high-level format: to clean up a floppy disk containing files you no longer need; as preparation before creating an emergency boot disk; or before installing a new OS.

Generally, when you change to a newer OS (for example, from Windows 98 to Windows 2000), you are given the option of *upgrading* rather than formatting your hard drive, or of doing what's called a *clean install*. Upgrading means that your data files, applications, and portions of Windows 98 will remain after Windows 2000 is installed on top of Windows 98. This is the fastest way to move from one OS to another, but it has drawbacks: Any viruses in the older OS can be passed to the new one; some outdated files will remain, taking up space and slowing down the OS; and obsolete OS accessory utilities might be left on the hard drive—still executable but not intended for use with the new OS. But most people opt for upgrading because its drawbacks are minor compared to the hassle of having to reinstall all the applications and data files.

Accidents Do Happen

What happens if you accidentally format the boot hard drive, or the drive hardware gets damaged in some way, or a virus zaps the boot sector? The result is that your computer cannot boot. Most of today's computers boot by default from a hard drive (C). If your boot hard drive fails for whatever reason, you'll have to go into your computer's Setup screen and choose the Boot from Diskette option. Then restart the machine with an emergency (or system) diskette in drive A. Techniques for recovering from hard drive failures are described in Lab 22.

Also note that if you have a system disk, all you need to do is insert the system disk and the PC will boot from that disk. A system disk is merely any disk containing some essential information transferred to it during the formatting process if you use the special /S switch, as in this example:

```
FORMAT A:/S
```

Most of today's popular operating systems offer you the option of creating an *emergency repair diskette* during the installation of the OS. This is a good idea. This disk contains the FAT, the boot sector, and the root directory, and it can sometimes make the process of recovering data from a damaged hard drive pretty simple. If the OS was installed by the computer manufacturer, you are usually given a few diskettes when you purchase the machine. One of these is usually labeled Boot Disk, and it is the emergency boot diskette you can use to reinstall the OS or otherwise deal with your boot hard drive's problems.

NOTE Sometimes it's possible to use the computer's Setup routine to switch the booting operation to your CD-ROM unit. If this option is available to you, you can then simply boot from the operating system CD that came with your computer—and restore your hard drive directly from the CD. According to recent reports, however, all versions of Windows (except the Server Edition of Windows 2000) shipped after April 1, 2000, from PC manufacturers who have direct license agreements with Microsoft will no longer include the traditional backup Windows CD. Instead, you get a "recovery CD" or a recovery "image" stored on your hard drive. Both of these new approaches to Windows recovery can be problematic; if your hard drive won't boot, a hard drive "image" isn't going to do you much good.

In this lab, you'll see how to format a diskette five ways:

- A simple DOS format
- A format that transfers the essentials of the operating system during the DOS formatting
- From Windows 95/98: a quick format, a full format, and a system-files format

By formatting a diskette with only the system files (the bare bones of the OS) included during the formatting, you are in effect creating your own emergency repair diskette. You can use it to boot into an elemental version of the OS (DOS or Windows) and thereby at least have a chance of recovering DOC files or other important data from a damaged boot hard drive.

WARNING Be very careful when using the FORMAT command. If you accidentally format your boot drive (usually C), you will have really shot yourself in the foot. You will have formatted your *boot hard drive* and thereby replaced the existing FAT, boot sector, and root directory with a new, empty FAT, boot sector, and root directory. In this lab we will format drive A—a new, blank floppy disk. *Do not format any hard drives in this lab!*

Exercise

To Format a Plain Diskette from DOS

1. From within Windows, choose Start ➤ Programs ➤ MS-DOS Prompt. A DOS window appears.

2. Place a brand-new diskette in drive A.

3. The DOS window is likely to display C:\, your boot hard drive's initial. Type this at the DOS prompt:

   ```
   C:\ FORMAT A:
   ```

   You will see a message asking you to press the Enter key when you've put a diskette in the A drive.

4. Press Enter. The OS checks the floppy disk's format and then displays the progress as the formatting operation lays down the new tracks, sectors, the FAT, boot sector, and root directory. When it's finished, you're asked whether you want to provide a volume label.

5. You don't have to provide a volume label, so just press Enter. You now see the details about the number of bytes available for file storage on this disk and the size of the allocation units. You're asked whether you want to format another diskette.

6. Type N and press Enter (because you're not ready to format another diskette just yet).

To Format a System Diskette from DOS (an Emergency Boot Diskette)

Follow the steps in "To Format a Plain Diskette from DOS," but in step 3 type this at the DOS prompt:

```
C:\ FORMAT A:/S
```

After the formatting is finished, you're told that the system was transferred onto this diskette, and that the system files used up nearly 400,000 bytes of the diskette's space.

To Format a Diskette from Windows

1. Double-click the My Computer icon.

2. In the My Computer window that opens, right-click the icon labeled 3½ Floppy (A:).

3. In the pop-up menu, select Format. The Format dialog box appears.

4. In the Format dialog box, click the Quick (Erase) Option button and the Display Summary When Finished check box.

5. Click the Start button. A high-level formatting takes place rapidly (as compared with the DOS format, which is always low-level). You're shown the details about the number of bytes available for file storage on this disk, and the size of the allocation units.

6. Click the Close button to shut the summary information window.

NOTE   A disk will not be formatted if it is currently open in either My Computer or Windows Explorer, or if any file on that disk is currently open in an application.

TIP   An alternative way to create a boot diskette is to click Start ➢ Settings ➢ Control Panel. When Control Panel opens, double-click the Add/Remove Programs icon. In the Add/Remove Programs dialog box, click the Startup Disk tab, and then click the Create Disk button.

To Format a System Diskette from Windows (an Emergency Boot Diskette)

Follow the steps in "To Format a Diskette from Windows," but in step 4 click the Full option button and the Copy System Files check box. This will cause a low-level format and will transfer the system files to the diskette. After the formatting is finished, you're told that the system was transferred onto this diskette and that the system files used up nearly 400,000 bytes of the diskette's space.

TIP   If you want to create a system boot diskette quickly, choose the Copy System Files Only option in the Format dialog box. This option relies on the tracks and sectors already marked off on the diskette, and it does not erase any files currently stored on the diskette.

Copyright @2000 SYBEX Inc.

Lab 16

DATE _____ NAME _____

1. Describe the two primary types of formatting.

_____

_____

_____

2. Define what an emergency boot disk is used for and how it works.

_____

_____

_____

_____

3. What is the difference between the FAT and the boot sector?

_____

_____

_____

_____

4. What is the quickest way to create a system diskette?

_____

_____

_____

Lab 17: Multiple Disk Partitions

Objectives for This Lab

Upon completion of this lab you will be able to

1. Recognize logical drives.

2. Create new logical drives.

Hardware & Software Requirements

Hardware: A working PC computer with DOS or Windows

Software: None for this lab

What to Read in the Book

Chapter 13, pages 616–29, *The Complete PC Upgrade & Maintenance Guide*, Mark Minasi, Sybex

Introduction

Partitioning divides a single hard disk into smaller logical units. There's still one physical drive in the computer, but the operating system sees it as two (or more) separate drives. The total size of the logical drives equals the size of the partitioned hard disk. Since IBM introduced the XT in 1983, hard disks on personal computers have required (or at least allowed) partitioning. Partitioning allows us to install different operating systems on the same computer.

The original reason for partitioning was to allow DOS and Unix to coexist on the same machine. Today, people use partitioning to install Windows 95 and Windows NT, or even Linux, on the same machine. If you plan to install Windows 95/98 and Windows 2000 on the same machine, you should install the two operating systems in different drives. Windows 2000 doesn't coexist well with previous versions of Windows on the same physical drive. Even if you partition a drive into two logical drives, Windows 2000 may take over the FAT of the drive on which Windows 95/98 is installed.

A second historical reason for partitioning was that Windows versions 3.*x* and earlier, as well as DOS, could not support large drives. As disk drives larger than DOS 3.3's maximum of 32MB became available in the mid-1980s, the only way to use that space was to partition the drive. Although the size limitations have effectively disappeared in Windows 95 and NT, space is still a good reason to partition a large drive into smaller logical ones: the smaller drives use disk space more efficiently. Windows manages disk space in small units, called *clusters*, and each cluster can belong to a single file. If the file is only 128 bytes long and the cluster size is 2048 bytes (2KB), then most of the cluster will be empty, because no other file can share the same cluster. The larger the disk is, the larger the size of the clusters, and therefore the more unused disk space.

NOTE   Partitioning isn't something you do in large hard drives, or in drives that you want to break into smaller logical units. To use a new drive, you must partition it. Even if it's a small drive that will be used as a single logical driver, you still have to partition it.

Using FDISK

To create a new partition, or change the existing partitions of a hard disk, you use the FDISK utility. Keep in mind that if you partition a disk by mistake, all the data is lost. Utilities such as the Norton Utilities can recover the original partition, but there's no guarantee that you'll recover all the data, and you should never partition a hard disk without good reason.

Hard disks are usually partitioned when we set up a new computer or install a new operating system (or two of them). If you must partition a disk that contains data, make sure that you back up all the data files first and *then* partition the hard disk. Applications must be installed after a successful partition.

Before using the FDISK program, let's review the basic terms you'll see in the FDISK screens:

Primary DOS Partition   This is the partition that contains DOS. Even if you're using Windows 95, you'll need a primary DOS partition on the system disk. The primary DOS partition will become drive C. The master disk becomes the first physical disk, and DOS requires that the first physical disk have a DOS partition. The other drives may contain extended partitions only.

Extended DOS Partition   The extended DOS partition consists of the space left on the drive after you have created the primary DOS partition. If you have a second hard drive, you can create an extended DOS partition without a primary DOS partition. Also, you can't create an extended partition on the first drive unless a primary partition exists already.

Logical DOS Drives   The extended DOS partition can be viewed as one or more logical drives. If you have a 1.2GB hard drive and you allocate 800MB to the primary DOS partition, you're left with a 400MB extended DOS partition. You can view this partition as a single 400MB logical drive (it will be drive D if you don't have a second hard drive), or two logical drives with a total size of 400MB, and so on.

Exercise

To View the Partitions

This procedure will not result in data loss and you can safely repeat it with a working computer. Just don't attempt to explore any options of the FDISK utility other than the one described here.

1. Boot with a DOS system disk or the Windows 95 Startup disk. If the partition was created with Windows 95, you must use the FDISK utility on the Windows Startup disk. Actually, if you want to view the partitions but not change them, you can open a DOS window and run FDISK.

2. At the DOS prompt, enter the FDISK command and press Enter:

   A:\> FDISK

3. When FDISK's main screen appears (Figure 17.1), select the option Display Partition Information by pressing 4. FDISK will display something like the following:

Partition	Status	Type	Volume Label	Mbytes	System	Usage
C:1	A	PRI DOS	Toolkit	1354	FAT16	100%

F I G U R E 17.1   The main FDISK screen

This tells you that the C drive is a single partition and uses 100% of the physical drive. The A in the Status column indicates that it's the active partition and it's a primary DOS partition. If you have a drive with multiple partitions, you'll see partition names like C:1, D:1, and so on. The letter is the name of the logical drive, and the number identifies the physical drive.

The system on the active partition is FAT16, which means you can install either DOS or Windows. If you're using the disk with Windows 95/98, you can convert FAT16 to FAT32. Note that after the conversion you can't go back to FAT16.

To Delete a Partition

This procedure and the following one assume that you have a spare hard drive, which you can partition and format at will. Do not use your computer's master drive to experiment with FDISK (or the FORMAT command, for that matter). If you delete an existing partition, there's no simple method to restore it. Apply the following steps to partition a new drive only, or a drive with a partition that contains no useful data.

1. Boot with a DOS system disk or the Windows 95 Startup disk. If the partition was created with Windows 95, you must use the FDISK utility on the Windows Startup disk.

2. At the DOS prompt, enter the FDISK command and press Enter:

   ```
   A:\> FDISK
   ```

3. When FDISK's main screen appears, press 3 to select Delete Partition or Logical DOS Drive. If you're using a new drive that hasn't been partitioned yet, you'll get a message to that effect. Follow the steps outlined in the next procedure to create a new partition first.

4. FDISK will display the following options:

   ```
   1. Delete Primary DOS Partition

   2. Delete Extended DOS Partition

   3. Delete Logical DOS Drive(s) in the Extended DOS partition

   4. Delete Non-DOS Partition
   ```

5. Select the first option by pressing 1. When prompted to enter the partition you want to delete, enter 1.

   If there's an extended DOS partition, you can remove it by selecting the second option in the Delete menu. Deleting an extended DOS partition is equivalent to deleting all the logical drives defined on this partition.

If you want to redefine the logical drives, you can delete them with the third option (`Delete Logical DOS Drive(s) in the Extended DOS Partition`) and then define new logical drives, as explained in the next procedure.

6. Press the Esc key to return to FDISK's main menu, and select 4 to see the partition information. If you have deleted both the primary and extended partition, you should see the message `NO PARTITIONS DEFINED`.

To Create a Partition

To create a new partition, you must first delete one or more existing partitions. Follow the steps of the preceding exercise to delete a hard disk's primary partition; then follow these steps to create a new primary partition. After creating a new partition, you must format it with the FORMAT utility as described in Lab 16. Do not repeat the following steps unless you have a spare drive with no useful data on it.

1. Boot with a DOS system disk or the Windows 95 Startup disk. If the partition was created with Windows 95, you must use the FDISK utility on the Windows Startup disk.

2. At the DOS prompt, enter the FDISK command and press Enter:

```
A:\> FDISK
```

3. When FDISK's main screen appears, press 1 to select the option Create Primary DOS Partition or Logical DOS Drive. You'll see the following menu:

```
1. Create Primary DOS Partition

2. Create Extended DOS Partition

3. Create Logical DOS Drive(s) in the Extended DOS Partition
```

If the disk has a primary partition, you won't be allowed to create a new one. Likewise, if the primary partition takes up all the space, you won't be allowed to create a new partition. If your disk doesn't contain a primary DOS partition, create a new one by pressing 1.

4. You'll be prompted to enter the size of the partition. Do not make the partition as large as the disk's size, because you may want to create an extended DOS partition later. Many users define a primary partition large enough for the operating system and the applications, and allocate the remaining space to an extended DOS partition that they use for storing data files.

5. Enter the size of the primary DOS partition and press Enter. FDISK will create the partition and then redisplay the main FDISK screen.

6. Select the second option in the initial menu to make the partition you just created the active one. Without an active partition, the drive cannot be started.

7. You can create an extended partition with the space that remains on the drive after creating the primary DOS partition. In the initial FDISK menu, select 1 (`Create DOS Partition or Logical DOS Drive`) and in the next menu select 2 (`Create Extended DOS Partition`). Give all the remaining space to the extended partition.

8. Now you're ready to create the logical DOS drives. Select 1 in the initial screen of FDISK, and in the next menu select 3 (`Create Logical DOS Drive(s) in the Extended DOS Partition`).

9. You'll be prompted for the size of the logical drive. Repeat steps 3 through 8 for each logical drive.

Lab 17

DATE _____ NAME _____

1. What utility do you use to manipulate the partitions of a hard disk?

_____

_____

2. When do you partition a disk drive?

_____

_____

_____

_____

_____

3. Write down the partition information for all the physical drives in your computer.

_____

_____

_____

_____

_____

4. Explain how DOS names partitions.

_____

_____

_____

_____

_____

Lab 18: Master/Slave Configurations

Objectives for This Lab

Upon completion of this lab, you will be able to

1. Add multiple hard drives to your computer.

2. Configure master and slave hard drives.

Hardware & Software Requirements

Hardware:

1. A working PC computer

2. A new hard drive

3. An antistatic wrist strap

4. A Phillips screwdriver

Software: None for this lab

What to Read in the Book

Chapter 11, pages 551–60; Chapter 13, *The Complete PC Upgrade & Maintenance Guide,* Mark Minasi, Sybex

Introduction

You already know how to replace an IDE/EIDE hard drive and how to prepare it for use with the FDISK and FORMAT utilities. Adding a second IDE/EIDE hard drive is nearly as simple, with one extra step (assuming you connect both drives to the same cable): You have to configure one of the drives as *master* and the other one as *slave.* You may find these terms confusing, because the two drives are equal in stature. (They will most likely be drives C and D.) Because the two drives are on the same IDE cable, there must be a mechanism that tells the BIOS which is which and prevents the two drives from competing with each other. This mechanism is the master/slave configuration and it applies to all pairs of drives installed on the cable. If the two drives are connected to different cables (that is, each drive is connected to its own hard drive connector on the motherboard), then both drives are master drives.

You may also have to install a third drive (or CD-ROM). In this case, you must use the second controller on the motherboard. The two hard drive connectors are usually labeled IDE1 and IDE2. IDE1 is the primary controller and IDE2 is the secondary controller. Again, this doesn't mean that the drives connected to the IDE2 connector are subordinate to the hard drives connected to IDE1; the names simply reflect the IDE connector to which they're connected.

To summarize, the motherboard has two hard drive connectors, and you can connect one or two drives to each one. The BIOS can easily distinguish the drives on either connector. The BIOS of a few old computers may not recognize two drives on each controller. If that's the case, you should update the BIOS, but it's doubtful you'll be able to find a new BIOS for the motherboard. Things get a little complicated with the two drives on the same data cable. Each drive has its own built-in controller, and the two controllers shouldn't fight each other. The solution is to disable the controller on one of the drives (by setting the jumpers on the back of the drive) and let the other drive's controller handle both drives. This is where the master/slave term comes from. The master drive's controller controls both drives on the same data cable.

So it's quite simple to add up to three hard drives in the same computer (or two hard drives and a CD-ROM drive) to the existing single drive. Your choice of which drive you connect to each cable doesn't make any difference, but there is a performance issue to consider. When a drive communicates with the CPU, the channel works at the capacity of the drive. The faster the drive, the faster the data is moved to and from the CPU. When the two drives communicate with each other, then they both operate at the speed of the slower drive. Hard drives are pretty fast and any mismatch in speed won't have a profound effect on the overall performance.

On the other hand, if you connect a CD-ROM and a hard drive to the same data cable, their mismatch in speed will degrade performance. If you have a game on a CD that needs to move volumes of data from the CD to the hard drive, both the CD-ROM drive and the hard drive will work at the speed of the slower device, which is the CD-ROM drive. If the two devices are instead connected to different controllers (different cables), then data is moved out of the CD at the speed of the CD-ROM drive, and into the hard drive at the speed of the hard drive. Thus, if you have a hard drive and a CD-ROM, you should connect them on two different connectors. A second hard drive must be connected to the same data cable as the first hard drive. If you decide to add a third hard drive, you must connect it to the same cable as the CD-ROM drive. This hard drive should be the slowest or least-used one.

Exercise

To Document the Hard Drives on Your PC

1. Turn off the computer, unplug all external cables, and open the case.

2. Write down the number and type of drives connected to the primary hard disk connector (IDE1).

3. Write down the number and type of drives connected to the secondary hard disk connector (IDE2).

4. Using the drawing in the motherboard's documentation, verify the names of the IDE connectors on the motherboard.

5. Close the computer, connect all cables, and turn it on. Start the BIOS Setup program by pressing the appropriate key(s) as the corresponding messages are displayed. In the BIOS Setup program, select the STANDARD CMOS SETUP screen.

6. Confirm that the drives connected to the primary and secondary controllers agree with your observations in steps 2 and 3.

To Install a Second Drive

In this procedure, you'll learn how to install a second hard drive in your computer. If your computer contains a second drive already, you can remove it and follow these steps to install it again.

If you're going to buy a second hard drive, you should consult the existing drive's documentation. Some old hard drives may be incompatible with certain drives from other manufacturers—they may not be capable of becoming slaves to other drives, and even the size of the second drive may be important. Because many compatibility issues aren't usually known when a device is manufactured, visit the manufacturer's site to see if any compatibility issues have come up. Alternatively, you can check at a site that discusses hardware issues, such as Tom's Hardware Site (www.tomshardware.com).

1. Turn off the computer, unplug all the cables, and open the case.

2. Locate all the hard drives (and CD-ROM drives) in the computer and their connectors. Label each connector and write down how it's connected to the corresponding drive. You may have to remove some of the existing drive's power and data cables to insert the second drive in its bay, so make sure you'll be able to reconnect all the cables when you're done.

   If your computer has a single hard drive and a CD-ROM drive on the same cable, continue with step 3. Otherwise, go to step 4.

3. Connect the CD-ROM drive to the second IDE connector with a new data cable (you may have to buy a new data cable, but most drives come with a spare).

With the CD-ROM drive out of the way, you can now connect the two hard drives to the same data cable, but not before you configure them as master and slave.

4. Disconnect the cables from the existing hard drive, remove the screws, and slide the drives out of their bays.

5. Examine the block of jumpers at the back of the drives. If the system has a single drive, then none of the jumpers is set. You'll probably see a cover sitting on one of the prongs, but it doesn't short any prongs. It's seated there but so far has been unused. You will use it now.

117

6. Figure 18.1 shows you how to set the jumpers on the master and slave drive. The slave drive must have its left jumper shortened.

7. You should configure the existing drive as slave and the new one as master. Consult the original drive's documentation to make sure that it will function as slave. If not, you'll have to set the new drive as the slave drive (only a few old drives will not slave to another drive).

8. While the drives are out of their bays, write down the specifications for each one. You may need the specs later, in case the BIOS can't auto-detect them.

9. At this point, you need a data cable with two 40-pin connectors at one end (you can purchase this cable at any computer store). Insert the drives partially in their bays, then plug in the data and power cables. Depending on the arrangement of the cables, you may have to place the new drive into the bay of the old one.

10. Now you can insert the drives fully into their bays and screw them in firmly. Notice that each drive is held in place by four screws, two on either side.

11. Start the computer and invoke the BIOS Setup program. Verify the connection of the drives on the primary and secondary controller, as well as their master/slave settings. The BIOS should see a master and a slave hard drive on the primary controller. If the computer has a CD-ROM installed, it will be the master drive on the second controller.

F I G U R E 18.1   Configuring drive jumpers

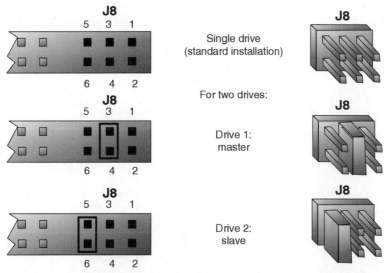

Configuring drive jumpers for a Western Digital AT-IDE 540MB hard disk drive

Lab 18

DATE _____ NAME _____

1. Explain the difference between a master and a slave hard drive.

   _____

   _____

   _____

   _____

2. How many hard drives are connected to your computer's primary and secondary controllers?

   _____

   _____

   _____

   _____

3. Explain how you would connect a CD-ROM drive to a computer with one hard drive. How would you connect two hard drives and a CD-ROM drive?

   _____

   _____

   _____

   _____

   _____

4. On a sheet of paper, draw the jumpers on the back of your drive(s). Indicate the settings that configure each drive as a slave.

5. What will happen if you switch the master and slave drives on a cable?

_____

_____

_____

_____

_____

_____

_____

Lab 19: Dual-Booting

Objectives for This Lab

Upon completion of this lab, you will be able to create a dual-boot system with Windows 98 and Windows 2000 (or NT 4 and Windows 2000) in separate partitions.

Hardware & Software Requirements

Hardware: A working PC computer with a hard drive divided into at least two partitions

Software: Two operating systems, which can include Windows 95, Windows 98, Windows 2000 Desktop or Server, and others

What to Read in the Book

Chapter 13, pages 616–18, *The Complete PC Upgrade & Maintenance Guide,* Richard Minasi, Sybex

Introduction

Some people like to use *dual-boot* machines. This means that when they start the computer running, they can select between two operating systems (OS).

As you learned in Lab 17, it's possible to divide a single hard drive into two or more logical drives (partitions). To the computer, each partition appears as a separate hard drive, with its own drive letter identity (C:\, D:\, E:\, and so on) and, if you wish, a separate OS: Windows 95, 98, 2000, Linux, NT, Unix, Windows 3.1, DOS, or others. (You can also have two separate hard drives with two operating systems, if you wish.)

Most dual-boot techniques require two separate partitions—one for each OS. (However, it is possible to place Windows 95 and DOS on a single partition.)

WARNING   If you ever make a low-level backup of a hard drive with a dual-boot system, be sure to back up the *entire* first track located at cylinder 0, head 0. Essential dual-boot information is stored in sectors 2 and 3 of this first track.

Why Use Multiple Operating Systems?

Why would someone want two operating systems for a single computer? Here are several reasons:

- You don't have any Windows 2000 drivers for your fax machine, for example, but you want to use 2000 as your main operating system. You therefore want to sometimes revert to Windows 98 to fax, but otherwise will spend most of your time in Windows 2000.

- You want to experiment with a new OS, such as Linux, but not abandon your tried-and-true Windows environment and all the software installed there.

- You need to test software that you've written yourself to verify the software's behavior in multiple operating systems.

- Some of your legacy software only works on DOS, so you want a clean, simple DOS drive.

- You are a member of a beta team and are testing the latest OS. By definition, this OS is unstable. You don't want to put all your eggs in that fragile basket, so as insurance you retain your older OS and its proven reliability. In this case, you might want to even consider using two hard drives, rather than partitioning one.

- You play games. One operating system is optimized for game software (Windows 98) and another is optimized for heavy-duty business and Internet work (Windows NT or 2000). You want to be able to switch between them.

- You're in charge of classrooms that instruct people how to use various operating systems.

- You want to use the same OS in two different languages.

Whatever your reasons, you can set up a dual-boot computer without too much hassle.

Exercise

To Create a Dual-Boot System with Windows 98 and Windows 2000

WARNING   Before you start, be sure you have at least two partitions (see Lab 17) on your hard drive, and that you have enough space. A minimal installation of Windows 98 requires at least 140MB free space on the hard drive, but if you install all possible options, it can use up almost 400MB. Windows 2000 requires a hard drive at least 2GB large, with at least 1GB of that drive free. Also, given the newness of 2000, you might want to install it on a second hard drive rather than a partitioned drive.

The following steps assume that you are currently running a Windows 98 system in one of the two partitions on your hard drive. (However, the same fundamental process described in these steps can be used to install Windows 2000 as a dual-boot system with a currently running NT 4 OS.)

WARNING   If you plan an NT 4/Windows 95 (or 98) dual-boot system, install Windows 95/98 *before* you install NT 4. During the Setup process, you'll be asked to give your computer a name. Do not use the same computer name that you used when installing the existing Windows 95 or NT 4 OS.

Also, if you expect you'll want to access files and applications located in the Windows 98 partitions when running Windows 2000 (and vice versa), format your disk partitions using FAT32. The alternative, NTFS, does not permit file sharing between partitions.

1. Run your Windows 2000 Setup CD. Right at the start, you're asked if you want to upgrade to Windows 2000 or install a new copy. Choose the latter option, `Install a new copy`. Note that the Setup screen comfortingly reassures you that you "can use multiple operating systems on your computer," which is precisely what you intend to accomplish.

WARNING   Unlike Windows 98, which *insists* on being installed in a directory named Windows, Windows 95 can be installed in a directory with any name you wish. However, it's advisable to install a Windows OS into the default directory suggested during installation. Some programs expect to find a directory named Windows and will misbehave if they do not.

2. Follow the Windows 2000 Setup instructions, installing Windows 2000 into your empty partition.

3. After Windows 2000 is installed, restart your computer.

4. A menu appears (in an old-style DOS screen) highlighting Microsoft Windows 2000 Professional (or whatever version of 2000 you're using). You'll also see `Microsoft Windows (98)` as a second option. You'll always see this menu whenever you reboot your system from now on.

   If you do nothing, Windows 2000 will start running in 30 seconds. If you press Enter, the computer boots into 2000 immediately. If you use your Up or Down arrow keys to move to the Microsoft Windows (98) option, you'll boot into that OS.

Note that you can change the default boot OS process by clicking Start ➤ Control Panel ➤ System. Click the Advanced tab, then click Startup and Recovery.

TIP   If you want to create a dual-boot system involving an OS other than the Windows 2000/Windows 98 combination, which is relatively straightforward, consider purchasing one of these utilities: V Communications's System Commander (www.v-com.com/productsscd.html); Masterbooter 2.9 (www.masterbooter.com/); or BootStart 5.51 (www.bootmenu.com/english). Each of these utilities assists you with installing different operating systems in the two hard drive partitions, allowing you to select your OS when you boot your computer in the future.

Lab 19

DATE _____ NAME _____

1. Describe what you must do before installing a dual-boot system.

_____

_____

_____

_____

_____

_____

_____

2. Name three reasons to create a dual-boot system.

_____

_____

_____

_____

_____

_____

_____

3. Why should you back up data files before creating a dual-boot system?

_____

_____

_____

_____

_____

4. If you need to access files and applications located in the Windows 98 partitions when running Windows 2000 (and vice versa), which file system should you use: the new NTFS or FAT?

_____

_____

Lab 20: Keeping Hard Disks in Good Shape

Objectives for This Lab

Upon completion of this lab, you will be able to

1. Defragment your hard drive to improve file storage and retrieval efficiencies.

2. Use the ScanDisk utility to get a report on the status of your hard drive's free, bad, and used space, and, optionally, test the surfaces of the hard drive to verify its integrity for data storage.

Hardware & Software Requirements

Hardware: A working PC computer with an installed hard drive

Software: The Windows ScanDisk and Disk Defragmenter utilities

What to Read in the Book

Chapter 16, pages 703–04, 706–13, *The Complete PC Upgrade & Maintenance Guide*, Mark Minasi, Sybex

Introduction

Windows stores your files in clusters—small zones of space on your hard drive. Large files are divided up and stored in many clusters. Usually, the operating system tries to store all the clusters for a particular file together, so they can be retrieved easily when you need to load the file into the computer's memory. That's not feasible after a while, however, because the disk gets fragmented. As you work with files, the OS must reuse the space freed by the deletion of files. Eventually the OS won't find enough contiguous space to store files and will write sections of a file in noncontiguous clusters. In order to retrieve the file, the OS must keep track of the clusters occupied by each file. This is the role of the FAT (File Allocation Table), a table that stores the addresses of the clusters that belong to each file. When the OS reads the file, it first looks up the FAT to find out which clusters to read and in what order. For more information on the FAT, see Lab 14, "The Hard Drive."

In much the same way that the OS organizes file clusters, Postal Service mail carriers spend the first 30 percent of each day sorting the mail for their route, putting all the letters for each house together. But on your hard drive, over time, clusters become scattered here and there on the surface of the disc. Each cluster contains a pointer (an address) for the next cluster—but you can imagine how inefficient it is for the drive head to have to skip around on the disk, gathering all the clusters for a file that's been *fragmented* in this fashion. It's as if the mail carrier dropped the bag, scattering the letters, and has to deliver them one by one, here and there, around town. Much too slow.

Windows includes a utility named Disk Defragmenter that corrects fragmentation. It moves the files around on the hard drive so the clusters are restored to contiguity, like pearls on a necklace. Files are saved and retrieved faster because the hard drive has much less work to do.

Another helpful Windows utility is ScanDisk, which is sometimes confused with the Defragmenter. Actually, ScanDisk (formerly known as CHKDSK when it was a DOS utility) doesn't work with the disk's files directly. Rather, it checks the FAT (file allocation table), which is the index of the contents of the drive. ScanDisk scans the FAT to count the number of clusters marked bad (that is, noted by other operations as unusable because of media flaws). ScanDisk itself doesn't automatically test the hard drive's surface for additional bad zones. However, you can enable the Thorough scan option, which does check for media problems, as you'll see later in this lab.

ScanDisk does the following work:

- It counts the used, bad, and available clusters.

- It verifies that directories and subdirectories are working properly.

- It compares each file's size with the number of clusters used by that file. If this comparison reveals a discrepancy between those two numbers, the file is marked as having "lost clusters."

- It ensures that each chain of clusters in the FAT is valid.

- Optionally, it checks the hard drive surfaces to locate any bad spots and marks them in the FAT.

ScanDisk runs automatically if you lose power accidentally or simply turn off the machine without going through the official Windows shutdown procedure. When you restart the machine, ScanDisk automatically runs and a message appears:

```
Because Windows was not properly shut down, one or more of your drives
may have errors on it
```

Exercise

To Defragment a Hard Drive

1. Choose Start ➢ Programs ➢ Accessories ➢ System Tools ➢ Disk Defragmenter. The Select Drive dialog box appears.

2. Click the Settings button in the Select Drive dialog box.

3. The default settings include the option to have your files rearranged on the hard drive so that the most-often-used files are placed in locations where they are most quickly retrieved. The Disk Defragmenter will defragment *all files*, but if you request this additional option, the process will take a little longer (not much). So go ahead and leave this option selected.

4. If you want to test the files and folders for errors, choose Check the Drive for Errors. This process, too, causes Disk Defragmenter to complete its job somewhat more slowly.

5. Click OK to close the Disk Defragmenter Settings dialog box.

6. Click OK to start the defragmentation process. You can click the Show Details button in the Disk Defragmenter progress dialog to see a visual display of the utility doing its work.

To Check the FAT for Problems

1. Choose Start ➤ Programs ➤ Accessories ➤ System Tools ➤ ScanDisk.

2. Choose the drive you want to scan, and select the Automatically Fix Errors option (otherwise, ScanDisk will halt every time it finds an error and ask you what to do). ScanDisk is a well-tested utility, and its default error-fixing schemes are reliable; the Automatically Fix Errors option is almost always your best choice.

3. Click the Thorough option if you want ScanDisk to test the surfaces of the disk drive to locate any unusable areas.

   ■ If you do select the Thorough option, click the Options button and specify if you want to test the entire drive, only the data area (your files), or only the system (the OS files).

   ■ You can also speed up the ScanDisk process by choosing to disable write-testing. (In this process, sample data is written to the media and then read back to see if it was correctly stored.)

   ■ The final option in the Thorough scan option is whether files with Hidden or System attributes should be moved if they are located in bad sectors.

TIP Some legacy (pre-Registry) applications expect to find information stored in hidden and system files in specific locations on the hard drive. This technique was used as a way of verifying the use of authorized (purchased) software. Such applications may fail to run if ScanDisk is forced to move these specialized files to a new location. Avoid disabling the option to repair hidden and system files (leave its check box unchecked) unless you have some really old applications that you are certain will fail as a result of ScanDisk's having moved a hidden or system file.

4. Click the Advanced button in the main ScanDisk dialog box, and you'll see a dialog box containing several more options. You can specify how you want ScanDisk log and summary files handled. You can choose what should be done with cross-linked files and lost fragments (pieces of files that cannot be identified as part of a FAT-linked file). You can also get a report of information such as invalid dates, times, filenames, name-length errors, and duplicate names. Finally, you can request that the host drive be checked first. Unless you have a reason to change these options, leave them set to their defaults.

5. When you're done setting the advanced options, click OK to close the dialog box and return to the main window of ScanDisk. Then click Start to start scanning your disk.

NOTE   You shouldn't start any other applications while ScanDisk is running, even though it's possible to do so. Applications create temporary files, which may cause ScanDisk to start scanning the disk all over again from the beginning.

Lab 20

DATE _____ NAME _____

1. What is a cluster?

_____

_____

_____

_____

_____

_____

_____

2. Describe fragmentation.

_____

_____

_____

_____

_____

_____

_____

3. What can ScanDisk do to help you keep your hard drive in good working order?

_____

_____

_____

_____

_____

_____

4. Name three options you can select in the Advanced dialog box of the ScanDisk utility.

_____

_____

_____

Lab 21: General Backup Techniques

Objectives for This Lab

Upon completion of this lab, you will be able to

1. Decide which kind of storage device makes the most sense in your situation.

2. Create a Backup Strategy sheet that suits your situation, and learn to follow it.

Hardware & Software Requirements

Hardware: A working PC computer with a tape drive, a Zip drive, a CD-RW drive, or a second hard drive

Software: For a tape drive, the drive's controller software; for a Zip drive, the Zip drive's backup-and-restore software; for a CD-RW drive, the drive's software

What to Read in the Book

Chapter 16, pages 691–98, *The Complete PC Upgrade & Maintenance Guide,* Mark Minasi, Sybex

Introduction

Do you faithfully back up your data? Or do you—like too many people—think you can rely on luck, plus the technological advances that have made hard drives highly reliable? Think again. They *are* highly reliable, but they are also heavily used, and they spin faster than you can imagine. Sooner or later you'll lose important data due to a disk crash, a virus, or some other catastrophic failure. At that point, those who don't back up are likely to finally join those of us who have a backup strategy and follow it without fail.

What to Back Up

Most people need not *mirror* their entire hard drive, creating an exact copy of it. This approach wastes time and media space because everything is saved twice—all of the applications are saved, along with the data generated by those applications. However, some mission-critical situations (such as Web servers) can require mirroring. If one hard drive fails, you can very quickly switch to its identical twin and keep on truckin'. For more on mirroring, see the section "Using a Second Hard Drive" later in this Lab.

What about applications? If your hard drive fails, reinstall your applications from their original CDs. With most of today's applications, restoring from a backup medium usually will not work (unless you are mirroring the entire drive). These applications store information in the Windows Registry, and necessary runtime libraries elsewhere, during the Setup process. So to install an application on a new drive, you must run its Setup program.

What you *do* need to back up is data: files generated by work you do with a spreadsheet, a database program, a word processor, or another program. Those files are precious if you value your time. You don't want them spinning into oblivion if your hard drive explodes.

Where to Back Up

In the old days, you could back up on floppy disks, but given the enormous size of today's data files, this is generally not a practical solution. It simply takes too long to keep feeding those floppies into the floppy drive, and you'd likely have to use lots of floppies to fully back up all your data.

Tape

Tape drives remain popular because they can store relatively large amounts of data, and they can be quite fast. DAT (Digital Audio Tape) drives are very efficient and inexpensive. Consider DAT if you're responsible for maintaining backups for a graphics department (graphics files are especially large) or another high-data-volume operation. DLT (Digital Linear Tape) is a 0.5"-wide cartridge format, available in sizes ranging from 20GB to more than 40GB. In addition to their speed, a second great advantage of DLT drives is their velocity: They boast transfer rates of 2.5MB per second.

Tape does have several disadvantages, however. For one thing, it's a serial storage medium. You cannot quickly move to any location in the tape—you must instead spool through it from start to finish to get to data stored at the end. Also, tape can require formatting, which can be time-consuming. Finally, the software that controls a tape drive may not work when you upgrade to a new operating system. If you do have huge backups, consider using either CD-RW or the emerging DVD media.

Zip or Jaz Drives

Removable media, such as the popular Iomega Zip and Jaz drives, are something like a hard drive "to go." You can treat them like floppy diskettes, inserting new Zip or Jaz disks as needed and storing them easily. But a Jaz disk holds as much as 700 times more data than a floppy. And like the hard drives they resemble, Zip and Jaz drives are fast. You can expect to back up a GB in around five minutes. The Zip/Jaz medium, though, seems to be approaching the end of its useful life—CD-R discs offer you 650MB for only pennies per disk, compared with the dollars per disk of the Iomega media.

CD-RW

CD-RW drives are simply CDs onto which you can save data (RW means Read/Write). These drives range in capacity from standard CD storage (650MB) up to the 5.2GB that a writeable DVD disk can hold. (Some DVD recorders can "only" record 3.9GB—avoid this older format.)

Using a Second Hard Drive

If you wish, you can also back up your data to a second hard drive. Hard drives have become relatively inexpensive. In Windows 95/98 you can back up by using the DOS XCOPY command; in Windows 95/98/NT/2000 you can drag and drop one drive's icon onto another's icon, or you can use the Disk Administrator to set up the drives as a mirror set. A mirror set means that two drives are virtually ganged together: Whenever any data is saved to one drive, the same data is simultaneously written to the other drive.

Exercise

To Choose a Hardware Device for Backups

Calculate the amount of data you currently back up.

- If your storage needs are typical (say, less than 650MB per backup), consider purchasing a CD-RW drive for its convenience and its low storage cost per byte.

- If your storage needs exceed 650MB, buy a DVD, DAT, or DLT drive because the media cost can be relatively low, these media are highly reliable, and the drives are fast. DVD recorders are just now becoming affordable.

- If you are working with a mission-critical application and must be able to switch quickly to a backup drive in case of a problem with your primary drive, buy a second hard drive and create a mirror set of the backup and primary drives.

To Create a Backup Strategy

1. Take a piece of paper and write "Backup Strategy" on it in large letters. Hang this paper on your wall to remind you of your promise to stick to a backup plan.

2. Decide how much work you are willing to redo in the event of a calamity.

TIP If you work eight hours a day on your computer, as we do, are you willing to repeat all eight hours of work when disaster strikes? If so, you can back up once a day. If you work only four hours a week on the computer, perhaps a weekly backup schedule is for you. But when you're responsible for backing up an entire office's output, you might consider running incremental backups more than once a day. Most applications include an auto-backup feature that can be a great help if you experience frequent power outages. You can specify the interval (every 15 minutes is good) at which the application will automatically save your work. In Word, for example, choose Tools ➢ Options, click the Save tab, and click the check box labeled Save Auto-Recovery Info Every *n* Minutes. Specify the interval in the text box. This won't provide you with a backup in the event of a hard-drive crash, but it will prevent you from having to repeat work if the power goes out.

---

3. If it's your job to back up several computers on a network, try to centralize the data—have all these workstations store their data on a single, central server. Also, teach the people on the network how to use the auto-backup features of their applications.

4. On your Backup Strategy sheet, write down the software you use to do the backup, any special instructions for using that software, and your backup schedule. If you back up weekly or monthly, perhaps you can write down the specific dates for each backup.

5. For backing up relatively large amounts of data, consider switching between full, incremental, and differential backups. If you choose this switching strategy, describe on your Backup Strategy sheet which type of backup is due on each date. Perhaps it makes sense for you to do a full backup once a month and incremental or differential backups every day.

NOTE An *incremental* backup saves only the files that have changed since the last full backup. A *differential* backup saves only the files that have changed since the last backup of any kind (either full or incremental). Backup software can detect which files have changed because each file contains an archive property that is set when that file is modified, and then turned off when that file is backed up.

6. Put your Backup Strategy sheet on your wall, where you'll see it. And each time you do a backup, initial and date it on the sheet. That way you'll always know precisely what's been backed up, how, and when.

Lab 21

DATE _____ NAME _____

1. Which backup medium is most cost-effective when you must back up large amounts of data, as in a graphics-intensive production department that generates many enormous files each day? And what are the drawbacks of this backup medium?

_____

_____

_____

_____

_____

_____

2. Describe the best backup technique to use for a mission-critical application, such as a Web server.

_____

_____

_____

_____

3. How do you determine how often you should back up your data?

_____

_____

_____

_____

4. What is the difference between differential, incremental, and full backups?

_____

_____

_____

_____

_____

Lab 22: Diagnosing and Fixing Hard Disk Problems

Objective for This Lab

Upon completion of this lab, you will be able to

1. Handle common drive errors.

2. Salvage a hard drive with bad sectors.

Hardware & Software Requirements

Hardware: None for this lab

Software: ScanDisk and Disk Defragmenter; Norton Utilities (optional)

What to Read in the Book

Chapter 16, pages 724–36, *The Complete PC Upgrade & Maintenance Guide*, Mark Minasi, Sybex

Introduction

Even if you take good care of a computer's hard drives and run the ScanDisk and Disk Defragmenter utilities frequently, there's no guarantee that the drives will be trouble free. There are two types of hard disk problems you will likely run into:

- Problems local to files or certain areas of the disk. These problems are easier to fix. Even if you lose some data, the majority of files will be unaffected.

- Problems in starting the disk, which are more difficult to fix. When the operating system can't see the hard disk at all, you may have to give up on this drive (or send it to a company that specializes in extracting every byte of information from a dead hard drive—for the right price of course).

The first sign of a hard drive's failure is a worrisome noise from the drive. The operating system or the BIOS is trying to write something to (or read something from) the disk, but it fails and keeps trying. You can't reproduce this type of failure at will, but many of you have heard this noise already. After a while, the operating system may successfully write the data on the location, but there will be a problem with your disk (you may not be able to read the data later, for example). If the operating system fails, it comes back with the infamous `Abort, Retry, Ignore` message. In Windows, the application will report a disk access error and probably give you a chance to retry (it may abort the save or read operation).

Many users will retry the operation. It rarely works because the operating system has already retried too many times (that's where the noise comes from). If you're trying to save a file from within an application, you should abort and try to save the data to another disk, or to a floppy. If you were trying to read a file, part of it has been lost for good.

Exit the application as soon as you can and try to copy the file you couldn't read to another location on the same, or another hard drive. The `COPY` command will copy everything it can, and when it hits the bad area will display the `Abort, Retry, Ignore` message. Select `Ignore` to skip the offending cluster. The copying process will continue with the remaining clusters. You'll end up with a file that contains most of the information, except for a cluster or two. You can either reconstruct the missing data or read as much as you can from the cluster that failed. The cluster that failed is made up of a number of sectors, and not all sectors have failed at once. You can use Norton Utilities or a similar program to read the cluster that failed. You should be able to retrieve the majority of the missing data. Then you can insert the data you retrieved from the failing cluster into the copy of the original file. Here again, you must work with a utility (such as Norton Utilities) that allows you to edit the contents of a file directly on the disk.

Many modern file types can be rendered useless even if a few bytes are missing, so recovering part of a lost cluster isn't going to be much help. This technique works with DOS text files, but most Windows applications in use today use proprietary formats for saving their data and you won't be able to fill in the missing information by hand.

Whether or not you had any luck saving the original file, you should immediately back up the entire drive. Do not postpone this, because the disk is on its way out. In this lab's "To Salvage a Hard Drive with Bad Sectors" exercise, you'll see how you can extend the life of a drive that starts to develop bad areas.

A general hard drive failure will probably scare users like no other computer disaster, but it may not be too difficult to fix. First, start the BIOS and make sure it can see the hard drive. The BIOS may have actually forgotten the hard drive's type (or misremembered it). If that's the case, enter the parameters and restart the computer. This may happen even if the CMOS battery is still good. (It's also a good indication that you must replace the CMOS battery.) If the computer displays error 1790 or 1791, you'll probably be able to fix it by specifying the proper parameters in the BIOS Setup program.

If the BIOS hasn't lost its parameters, open the computer and make sure no cables have come loose. Consider yourself lucky if this fixes the problem, but it does happen with many computers. Even desktops that haven't been moved in months have had drive cables come loose. Also try another set of cables, and try connecting the drive to the second EIDE connector on the motherboard.

If the drive is powered and all your attempts have failed, boot from the floppy drive and try to see the failing hard drive. If you can access the drive, get the data out while you can. Then you can try to partition or format the drive, but your first priority is to get the data out. Then reinstall the drive and if it fails, throw it away.

Exercise

To Fake Errors on the Hard Drive

This procedure simulates the behavior of a computer with a hard drive failure. Even though we won't do anything destructive to the hard drive, you should back up the hard drive(s) in the computer before starting the exercise.

1. Start the BIOS Setup program (as explained in Lab 9) and change the type of the C drive. Set it to None so that the BIOS won't find a bootable hard drive. Before you change any parameters, write down the current values.

2. Restart the computer and write down the error message displayed by the BIOS.

3. See if you can start the computer with a floppy and access the drive.

4. Restart the computer, start the BIOS Setup program, and restore the drive's parameters (or use the IDE Hard Disk Autodetect option). Save the settings and restart the computer.

5. Now turn off the computer. Unplug the drive's data cable, but leave the power cable plugged in. By the way, you should *never* do the opposite (don't leave the data cable on the hard drive without the power cable).

6. Plug all the cables into the back of the computer and turn it on. Write down the error message displayed by the BIOS.

7. Open the computer again, reconnect the data cable, and make sure the computer comes on as before. If the BIOS can't see the drive, enter the BIOS Setup program and set the drive's parameters.

To Salvage a Hard Drive with Bad Sectors

The following procedure shows you how to make the most of a disk that has developed bad sectors. Examine the steps of the procedure and understand how you would repeat them in a real world scenario. Of course, you can't apply this procedure to a hard drive that is working properly.

1. If you have reason to believe that the hard drive has developed bad clusters, you must first confirm your suspicions with a utility such as ScanDisk. Launch ScanDisk by clicking the Start button and

choosing Programs ➤ Accessories ➤ System Tools ➤ ScanDisk. Select the Thorough option so that ScanDisk will scan the surface of the disk.

2. If the hard drive contains bad clusters, ScanDisk will mark them as bad and will not use them.

3. If the hard disk is still under warranty, you can return it to the manufacturer and they must replace it.

4. If it's not under warranty, you can still use the disk, but it won't get any better. Chances are it will develop more bad clusters and the recovery process will have to be repeated. Every time a sector goes bad, you risk losing useful data. When this happens, it's time to replace the drive. Before you throw away the old drive, however, examine the location of the bad sectors. There's a good chance that the bad sectors have appeared at the beginning of the disk and that they're contiguous, too. Some areas of the disks are being used much more often than others and so are more likely to fail first. Two such areas are the Windows Swap file and the FAT.

5. You can estimate the location of the bad sectors by looking at the display produced by the Disk Defragmenter as it progresses through the disk. Bad clusters are marked with a red stripe. See if the majority of the bad sectors are at the beginning of the drive.

6. If that's the case, you can "throw away" part of the drive and keep the rest. To do so, move all the data files from the failing drive to the new one.

   If you haven't yet installed a new drive, back up your data files to another medium. Then partition the old drive into two logical drives with FDISK. Make the first partition as small as possible, but also make sure all the bad sectors are in this partition. Give the rest of the drive to the second partition.

7. Your system will now have two extra drives; let's say they're drives D and E. Ignore drive D because it's the one with the bad sectors; use the E drive. It's recommended that you install applications in this drive, so that even if it fails, too, you won't lose important data. You can always reinstall your applications.

Lab 22

DATE _____ NAME _____

1. What's the first thing you'll do when your computer doesn't start because of a general hard drive failure?

_____

_____

_____

2. What tool will you use to find out the location of the bad clusters? Is it worth fixing them?

_____

_____

_____

_____

3. What's the first thing to do when you discover that the hard drive has developed a new bad cluster?

_____

_____

_____

_____

4. What tool will you use to mark bad areas on the disk?

_____

_____

Lab 23: Installing a SCSI Adapter

Objectives for This Lab

Upon completion of this lab, you will be able to

1. Decide if the SCSI I/O port would be a better choice than alternative ports for attaching peripherals to your system.

2. Install a SCSI card.

3. Set the ID number for any SCSI peripheral.

4. Terminate the SCSI connection.

Hardware & Software Requirements

Hardware:

1. A working PC computer

2. A SCSI card

3. An antistatic wrist strap

4. A Phillips screwdriver

Software: Drivers and any other software provided by the manufacturers of any SCSI peripheral you want to attach to the SCSI adapter (also sometimes called a *host adapter*).

What to Read in the Book

Chapter 12, pages 562–85, *The Complete PC Upgrade & Maintenance Guide*, Mark Minasi, Sybex

Introduction

The Small Computer Systems Interface (SCSI, or "scuzzy" to you) made its debut in the mid-1980s as a result of envy. Macintosh users have always boasted about the superiority of their SCSI connectors (which are faster than standard serial or parallel ports, and you can daisy-chain multiple devices to a single SCSI port). Envying their Mac compatriots, some IBM PC users hoped they, too, could use

SCSI-type ports, rather than the IDE standard, to attach peripherals—especially hard drives—to their computers.

Their wish came true when SCSI for PCs was formally introduced in 1986. Alas, SCSI's early promise has faded because it failed to standardize; most every hardware maker seems to think it knows best how to implement SCSI. Therefore, proprietary interface designs, varying device drivers, varying SCSI versions, and even several different kinds of connectors all have made compatibility among SCSI devices merely a botched ideal.

SCSI does have its attractions, though:

- It can use short cables, reducing noise levels.
- Some SCSI peripherals feature built-in diagnostics.
- You need only one controller card rather than a separate card for each peripheral.
- It is fast, fast, fast.
- You can daisy-chain multiple peripherals to the same connection.

So if you're responsible for maintaining a SCSI-based machine, or if you want to upgrade from IDE to take advantage of SCSI's benefits, this lab is for you. You'll learn how to install a SCSI host adapter (the translator between SCSI peripherals and your computer's CPU and memory). If you're thinking of upgrading, though, we suggest you seriously consider USB or Firewire rather than SCSI (see sidebar).

The USB and Firewire Challengers to SCSI

USB (Universal Serial Bus) is a relatively new connector, just now becoming common on most desktops and portables. It offers some of the same features as SCSI, such as daisy-chaining, but in several ways is a serious improvement on SCSI.

For example, USB eliminates the need for an adapter card. It also permits hot connecting (you can plug something into a USB connection without turning off your machine's power). USB's features and speed are most useful with such peripherals as printers, mice, keyboards, audio devices, joysticks, telephones, and scanners. Featuring a 12MB-per-second transfer rate, USB can also comfortably handle digitizers, ISDN phone lines, and some MPEG-2 video peripherals.

Note that SCSI is actually faster than USB. SCSI transfers as much as 40MB per second. However, SCSI is in most respects a technology in decline. Some of its weaknesses are that it doesn't permit hot connecting; it requires that you assign each device its own address; and it needs a terminator for the last device in the daisy-chain. And above all, manufacturers have failed to agree on a SCSI standard, so there is much unfortunate incompatibility between SCSI devices.

Firewire, another new serial bus plug-and-play device connection system, can handle far greater data-transfer rates than USB—up to a blazing 400MB per second. (Today's devices "only" reach between 100 and 200MB per second, but 400MB is a realistic future goal.) These rates are most beneficial when attaching ultra-high-speed peripherals such as DVD player/recorders and digital motion video cameras.

At this time, there isn't much Firewire hardware available, and there are rumors of an improved version of USB that could challenge Firewire. Nevertheless, experts predict that USB and Firewire will happily coexist, each serving a different need.

Exercise

To Install a SCSI Card

1. Ensure that the SCSI card is compatible with the computer and all peripherals you intend to attach to the card. Here are the features to look for to ensure compatibility:

   - Check the cable standard (SCSI-1, SCSI-2, or SCSI-3, and beware of variations even *within* each of these three "standards").

   - Make sure that any external SCSI devices you intend to daisy-chain can be located close together. SCSI cables must not be longer than a few feet, or the connection will fail.

   - Check ID compatibility. Every attached SCSI peripheral must have a unique SCSI ID (from 0 to 7; or for SCSI-3 single-channel devices, the ID can range from 0 to 15).

   - Determine the termination style of each peripheral. (Termination is required at each end of a SCSI daisy-chain of devices, but there are two types—active and passive termination. Worse, some peripherals have no built-in termination; some have optional termination; some even insist on being the terminator device.)

   - If you are daisy-chaining, ensure that each external SCSI device you want to put into the chain has *two* SCSI connectors.

2. If you have an internal SCSI device, attach its cable to the connector at the top of the SCSI card.

3. Insert the SCSI card into a PCI slot in your computer.

4. Insert the plug from the first external SCSI device in the daisy-chain, into the connector on the back of the SCSI card.

5. Adjust the ID number(s) for the external device(s). There is a device ID number adjuster on each external SCSI peripheral, allowing you to change the ID. Usually it's best to use the manufacturer's default setting (if possible). Also note that settings 0 and 1 are not allowed. And Pin 1, the red pin on the 50-pin SCSI cable, must be closest to the power supply.

6. Locate the SCSI peripheral at the far end of the daisy-chain, and ensure that it is terminated. There may be a termination switch on the peripheral, or you may have to attach a terminator plug; if not, there should be some other method of termination. Check the device's instruction booklet if you need help.

Lab 23

DATE _____ NAME _____

1. List four benefits of using SCSI as compared to using the traditional IDE connection.

_____

_____

_____

_____

_____

_____

_____

2. What are the primary drawbacks to SCSI, and why are they problems?

_____

_____

_____

_____

_____

_____

_____

3. How do you terminate a SCSI daisy-chain, and how do you assign an ID number to a SCSI peripheral?

_____

_____

_____

_____

_____

4. List the steps you should take to ensure compatibility between the SCSI card you're installing and the SCSI peripherals you plan to attach to it.

_____

_____

_____

_____

_____

Lab 24: Installing a Video Board

Objectives for This Lab

Upon completion of this lab, you will be able to

1. Install a new video board.

2. Set up the properties of the video board.

Hardware & Software Requirements

Hardware:

1. A working PC computer with Windows 95/98

2. A video board with cables and mounting hardware

3. An antistatic wrist strap

4. A Phillips screwdriver

Software: The video driver supplied with the board

What to Read in the Book

Chapter 23, *The Complete PC Upgrade & Maintenance Guide,* Mark Minasi, Sybex

Introduction

The video board, which is responsible for displaying information on the computer's monitor, is one of the simplest devices in a computer, at least to set up. The video board is basically a computer within the computer, because it has its own processor, memory, and even its own BIOS. Fortunately, you don't have to program it. The operating system communicates directly with the video board and stores the image (bitmap) to be displayed on the monitor in the board's memory. Advanced applications do not create the bitmap; rather, they send commands to the board's processor, which executes them and creates the bitmap to be displayed. No matter how the information gets there, it must be first stored in the board's memory from where it's mapped on the monitor.

The two characteristics of the video board are its resolution and color depth. The *resolution* is the total number of pixels the video board can display on the monitor; and the *color depth* is how many colors it can display. Of course, the monitor should also be able to keep up with the video board.

Most monitors today can display up to 1280×1024 pixels and nearly 16 million colors. The most common resolutions for desktop monitors are 800×600 and 1024×768. To display 256 colors at these resolutions, the board's memory must have at least 480,000 or 786,432 bytes, respectively, because you need one byte per pixel. To display true color at the same resolution, the board must have three times as much memory, because true color requires three bytes per pixel. In general, you can't increase both the resolution and number of colors. Depending on the amount of memory on the video board, you may have to lower the resolution in order to increase the number of colors, or vice versa. For a list of the available display cards and the resolutions and color depths they support, see Table 23.1 in *The Complete PC Upgrade & Maintenance Guide*.

Modern video boards use several megabytes of memory because they use memory to render complicated three-dimensional graphics, not just the bitmap to be displayed. You can also upgrade today's boards by installing additional memory.

While we're discussing their memory requirements, let's review the memory types used with video boards. The most common type of memory is the dual-ported memory, or VRAM (Video RAM). The characteristic of this memory type is that it can accessed by two chips at once. The CPU is writing data while the imaging chip is reading the data and sending them to the DAC (Digital to Analog Converter), which updates the monitor. The DAC converts the image from its digital form to an analog form suitable for display on a monitor. Many video boards use WRAM (Window RAM), which allows the CPU to fill blocks of memory with a few commands. Newer graphics boards use Synchronous Graphics RAM (SGRAM), which is considerably faster than VRAM; and Double Data Rate RAM (DDR SDRAM), which isn't faster than VRAM but moves twice as much data per cycle.

Troubleshooting Tips

When the monitor doesn't come on, there are two possible sources of malfunction, which you must eliminate one at a time.

First, the monitor itself: If the monitor is dead, its LED won't come on as the computer starts. Before you replace the monitor, however, make sure that the computer is working. If the monitor is powered from the computer and the computer's power supply is dead, you need only replace the computer's power supply. If the computer's LEDs turn on and off as the operating system loads, then you most likely have a dead monitor.

The other possible culprit is, of course, the video board: If the monitor's LED comes on but nothing appears on the screen, the problem is with the video board. Make sure the monitor's cable is plugged in, and then replace the video board. To figure out quickly whether the video board is working or not, start the computer in DOS mode (either with the recovery diskette or by pressing F8 while Windows loads). If you hear one long and two short beeps at startup, this is the BIOS telling you that the video board isn't working.

The most common problem with video boards is that users change either the resolution or the monitor's refresh rate to a value that the monitor can't support. When this happens, the monitor displays something that looks like the desktop (or the DOS prompt) in bands, or it repeats the same bitmap across the screen. You'll need to shut down the computer with the keyboard, and then restart in Safe mode by pressing F8. The Safe mode uses the lowest settings and you'll be able to restore the video board's settings. Lower either the resolution or the refresh rate.

Finally, you may experience intermittent problems with some video boards. Suspect the video aperture, and see if a user has turned it on. (Some video boards use system memory to store the image, in order to speed the display operation. This memory is called aperture memory.) In some cases, the wrong setting for the video aperture may cause Windows to crash. You can change the settings of the video aperture from within the BIOS Setup program, which is described in Lab 9.

NOTE The following procedures assume that you have a video board installed on your computer. Many computers, however, include all the video circuitry on the motherboard. You can still set up the video properties, but what if you want to install a new, more advanced video board on one of these computers? The video circuitry on the motherboard can't be removed, but you can disable it. Motherboards with built-in video have a special jumper on the board, which you can set to disable the on-board video circuitry. Consult the motherboard's documentation to find out the location of the jumper and then set it accordingly. Also, many of today's motherboards allow you to disable the on-board video card through the BIOS, so be sure you check the documentation to find out whether you have to set a jumper or go through the BIOS Setup program.

Exercise

To Remove the Video Board

1. Disconnect all peripherals and open the computer's case.

2. Determine whether the graphics adapter is on the motherboard. If the computer has a separate video board, go to step 4.

3. If the graphics adapter is on the motherboard, you must locate the jumper that disables it. Consult the motherboard's documentation and set the jumper accordingly.

4. Remove the screw that holds the video board on the case and then lift the board out of its slot. Now go to the next procedure, "To Add a New Video Board."

To Add a New Video Board

1. Insert the new board into the slot and screw it down.

2. Video boards commonly have an internal connector, known as the *feature connector*, which is used to connect the board to other video devices in the computer, such as a TV tuner. If you have one of those devices and your board has a feature connector, connect the feature connector to the appropriate board by following the manufacturer's instructions.

3. Close the computer, reconnect all cables, and turn it on.

4. Windows should detect the new card and set up the appropriate drivers. If it cannot identify the card, Windows will treat it as a generic VGA card with a resolution of 640 × 480 at 16 colors. If Windows detects the new card but has no native driver for the board, Windows will prompt you for the diskette with the manufacturer's drivers.

5. Insert the diskette or the CD that came with the video board and let Windows continue with the installation of the drivers.

6. If Windows can't detect the new device (and treats it as a standard VGA card), locate a SETUP.EXE or INSTALL.EXE program on the CD and run it. The appropriate drivers will be installed, and the next time you turn on the computer you'll be able to adjust the video board's properties (this process is described later in this lab).

To Remove Old Video Board Drivers

To make sure that the new video drivers will not conflict with any existing drivers, uninstall the existing drivers.

1. Right-click My Computer on the desktop, and from the shortcut menu select Properties. When the System Properties dialog box appears, click the Device Manager tab.

2. On the Device Manager tab, locate the Display Adapters item and click the plus sign in front of it. You should see the name of the display adapter you just installed, and perhaps the names of other adapters that were not properly uninstalled. Select any obsolete adapter name and click Remove.

3. Repeat the process for all video adapters you no longer need.

To Set the Video Board's Properties

1. Right-click on the desktop and from the shortcut menu select Properties. When the Display Properties dialog box appears, select the Settings tab. Here you can adjust the resolution of the display as well as the number of colors.

2. Increase the resolution of the display as much as you can. Depending on the new board's properties, you may be able to reach a resolution of 1280×1024, or even higher. Notice that as you increase the resolution, the number of colors is reduced automatically. Likewise, if you increase the number of colors, the computer will lower the resolution to accommodate the specified number of colors. If the video board has the maximum amount of memory, it won't make any adjustments. Most video boards come with 2–4MB of RAM and can't display the maximum number of colors at the maximum resolution.

3. If the monitor can't display the resolution you've specified, you'll see a badly distorted image on the monitor. Don't press a button for 15 seconds, and Windows will cancel your changes and return to the previous resolution. This will happen only if you have requested that the new settings are applied without restarting. If you see a warning to the effect that the new settings can't be applied before the computer is restarted, go ahead and restart it. If the image on the screen is scrambled, restart the computer again and this time press F4 to start the computer in the so-called Safe mode. Windows will start the computer with a resolution of 640×480, and you can repeat the process to set the display properties to a resolution that's supported by the monitor. The new resolution will take effect the next time you start Windows in regular mode.

TIP It's also possible that you may have to change the type of the monitor, if it's not a Plug-and-Play monitor. To do so, click the Advanced button on the Settings tab of the Display Properties dialog box. On the new dialog box select the Monitor tab and you will see the type of monitor currently installed. This is the type of monitor Windows thinks is installed, and it may be different from the monitor actually being used. Select the proper monitor type in this tab (you may be asked to provide a disk or CD to install the correct files) and click the OK button twice to close the Display Properties dialog box.

TIP Another option you can set in the Advanced Display Properties dialog box is the Refresh rate. This rate is expressed in Hz (cycles per second) and it determines how frequently the screen is updated. The higher this value, the crisper the image on the screen. Practically, any value over 100 Hz is a very good refresh rate.

Lab 24

DATE _____ NAME _____

1. How much memory is on your video board?

_____

_____

2. What's the highest resolution you can display on your monitor? Can the video board display higher resolutions that your monitor can't handle?

_____

_____

_____

3. Explain the relationship between resolution and number of colors.

_____

_____

_____

_____

_____

_____

4. What is the refresh rate? Do good monitors have a small or a large refresh rate?

_____

_____

_____

_____

_____

Lab 25: Installing a CD-ROM, CD-RW, or DVD Drive

Objectives for This Lab

Upon completion of this lab, you will be able to

1. Decide on the best position in the drive bay to install a CD or DVD drive.

2. Install a new or replacement CD or DVD drive.

3. Install a DVD decoder board.

Hardware & Software Requirements

Hardware:

1. A working PC computer

2. A CD-ROM, CD-RW, or DVD drive (and possibly a DVD decoder card)

3. A Phillips screwdriver

4. An antistatic wrist strap

Software: Drivers and any other software provided by the manufacturers of the drive you install. We recommend you also look at any README.TXT files that come with the hardware or that are included when you download drivers from the Internet.

What to Read in the Book

Chapter 32, pages 1331, 1337–38, 1343–47, *The Complete PC Upgrade & Maintenance Guide*, Mark Minasi, Sybex

Introduction

Installing a CD-ROM, CD-RW, or DVD (Digital Versatile Disk) drive is similar to installing a hard drive. However, you should carefully read any drive's instruction booklet to see if there are special instructions. In this lab, you'll install a typical CD-ROM drive. CD-RW and DVD drives are installed essentially the same way. (These drives are backward-compatible. A CD-RW or DVD drive can also be used as a standard CD-ROM.)

NOTE DVD is the next removable (and potentially backup) medium coming down the pike. DVD will eventually replace CDs, just as CDs have replaced floppy disks. DVD discs are the same size as CD-ROM discs, but instead of the CD's silvery rainbow prisms, a DVD tends toward gold, with a holographic prism effect. However, it's the storage capacity that makes DVD the new medium of choice. These discs can store more than 26 times as much data (17GB) as CD-ROMs (650MB)—we're talking MB (millions) versus GB (billions) here. Inevitably, writeable DVD technology will soon make its appearance as an affordable backup medium, as well. (Current "DVD-RAM" drives, as they are confusingly called, cost around $700 and store a little more than 5GB.)

There are three primary differences between installing an ordinary hard drive and installing a CD or DVD drive:

- A hard drive is installed from within the computer's case, but a CD/DVD drive must be accessible to users so they can insert and remove the discs. As a result, when installing a hard drive you push it into the drive bay from within the computer's case, but you push a CD/DVD drive in from the outside of the front of the computer's case.

- CD/DVD drives play audio through the sound card and thence to the computer's speakers. A cord must be connected between the CD/DVD drive and the computer's sound card.

- A DVD drive may require that a *decoder card* be installed in an empty PCI slot. This card provides hardware-based MPEG decoding. DVD movies are MPEG encoded and cannot be viewed without decoding. It's possible to use software to decode MPEG, but hardware-based decoding is superior (faster, and therefore produces a sharper image). Some DVD drives, however, use software-based decoding.

TIP One implication of CD/DVD drives' accessibility to the user is that you must decide the order in which you stack them in the case. The best approach is to put a CD or DVD drive on top (where the user can easily exchange the CDs), put the Zip drive (if any) just below the CD/DVD, and finally, lowest in the drive bay, install the hard drive(s). Often a Zip disk is ejected from its drive but still sits in the drive, protruding a couple of inches out from the case. You don't want the idle Zip disk blocking your access to the CD tray when you try to remove or insert a CD from the CD drive. Keep in mind, however, that the increasing popularity of CD-RW drives is likely to push Zip drives into history. Zip disks are much more expensive than CDs (dollars versus pennies), and Zip disks hold less data.

Exercise

To Install a CD or DVD Drive

1. Turn off the computer, unplug all external cables, and open the case.

2. If a hard disk drive or Zip drive is currently occupying the uppermost space in the drive bay, unscrew that drive and move it down a space. You want to make room at the top of the bay to install your CD/DVD drive where the user can most easily access it. (The exception to this rule is the floppy diskette drive, which usually sits at the very top—more for historical than practical reasons. You may not be able to demote the floppy drive from its top position if it won't go lower. Some of them are built right into the case itself.) If you're upgrading from a CD drive to a CD-RW or DVD drive, remove the existing CD drive from the computer.

3. If the data cable and audio cable are not yet attached to the computer and audio card, plug both cables into the CD/DVD drive. The topmost position in the drive bay is usually cramped, so it's sometimes best to attach the cables to the CD/DVD drive before seating the drive into the drive bay. However, if you're replacing an existing CD drive, wait until step 6 to attach the cables.

NOTE   The data cable should be attached with its pin 1 positioned nearest the power connector. Pin 1 on the cable is indicated by a red (or dark) stripe. Simply make sure that the cable's stripe is facing nearest the power receptacle on the back of the drive. (See Figure 25.1; the power receptacle is the 4-pin connector on the right side.)

F I G U R E   25.1   Receptacles on the back of a DVD drive; CD drives are functionally identical

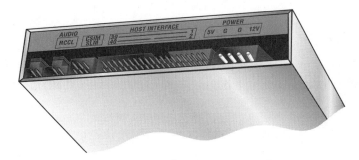

4. If you've attached the data and audio cables to the CD/DVD drive, feed them now into the drive bay (from the front of the computer) as you gently slide the CD/DVD drive into the drive bay.

5. Secure the CD/DVD drive to the drive bay using the supplied screws. Do not overtighten the screws.

NOTE   Some newer computers use a kind of metal sled that's screwed to the bottom of a CD/DVD or hard drive. The unit is simply pushed into the drive bay where the sled snaps into place, securing the drive in the drive bay. If your machine features this snap-in sled, you'll attach the sled in step 5 rather than securing the drive to the bay with screws into the sides of the drive.

6. Insert the power connector into the CD/DVD drive, paying attention to the position of the angled corners of the power plug. Ensure that the angled corners of the plug line up with the angled corners in the drive's receptacle. If you haven't yet attached the data and audio cables, do so at this time.

7. Set the CD/DVD's control block to the slave position. (See the manufacturer's instructions for the location and position of this switch or set of jumper plugs.)

TIP If you're using Windows 98 or another OS that features Plug and Play (PnP), and your CD/DVD drive is PnP compatible, you'll find *three* jumpers or a three-position switch on the back of the CD/DVD drive: Master/Slave/PnP. Do not set the jumpers or switch to Master or Slave. Use the third option, PnP, so that the OS can detect the drive and automatically define its relationship to any other drives in the system.

---

8. Attach the data cable to the secondary IDE connector on your motherboard, if it isn't already attached.

9. Plug the other end of the audio cable (the end attached to the CD/DVD drive) into your sound card, if necessary. See the sound card's instructions for the location of its CD audio receptacle. If you find two CD audio receptacles, use the one named "In 1" or some other label involving the number 1. Check the card's instructions if necessary.

To Install a DVD Decoder Card

In this procedure, you'll insert a DVD decoder card into the system's video stream. This means you must switch your monitor's cable from its classic location in the back of the video board to a receptacle on the back of the DVD decoder card. You'll also plug a cable between the DVD decoder card and your video card.

1. Find an empty PCI slot and seat the DVD decoder card in that slot.

2. An audio cable and a video feed-through cable are packaged with the DVD decoder card. Insert the mini-DIN plug on the video feed-through cable into the receptacle on the DVD decoder card.

3. Unplug your monitor's cable from the back of your video card and plug it into the receptacle on the back of the DVD decoder card.

4. Plug the 15-pin D-connector on the other end of the video feed-through cable into the video output receptacle on the back of your video card (the receptacle you made vacant in step 3).

5. Attach the audio cable between the DVD decoder card and your sound card, as described in the DVD decoder's installation manual.

Lab 25

DATE _____ NAME _____

1. List the three primary differences between installing an ordinary hard drive and a CD or DVD drive.

_____

_____

_____

_____

_____

2. Where should you position a CD or DVD drive in the computer's drive bay, and why?

_____

_____

_____

_____

_____

3. How do you determine which way to plug in a data cable?

_____

_____

_____

_____

_____

4. Describe the two places where you must plug in the video feed-through cable when installing a DVD decoder card.

_____

_____

_____

Lab 26: The Serial and Parallel Ports

Objectives for This Lab

Upon completion of this lab, you will be able to

1. Configure the serial ports on your computer.

2. Communicate with devices connected to your computer's ports.

Hardware & Software Requirements

Hardware: A working PC computer

Software: None for this lab

What to Read in the Book

Chapter 3, pages 216–18; Chapter 6, pages 349–62; Chapter 19, *The Complete PC Upgrade & Maintenance Guide*, Mark Minasi, Sybex

Introduction

The serial and parallel ports enable your computer to communicate with some of the most common peripheral devices: printers, backup devices, and modems. The main difference between serial and parallel ports is that serial ports move information one bit at a time, and parallel ports move information one byte at a time. In addition, the serial port is an asynchronous device; it uses the start and stop bits to regulate the flow of data. The parallel port on the other hand transmits data synchronously; it uses a clock signal to regulate the flow of data. Parallel ports are used with relatively fast devices such as printers and backup devices; serial ports are used almost exclusively with modems. There was a time when printers connected to the serial port, but these printers are long extinct.

Parallel ports are simpler to manage, because all manufacturers follow the same conventions. When it comes to serial ports, however, manufacturers use different connectors and you may have to build your own cable to connect two devices. The serial port is on its way to extinction, being slowly replaced by the newer USB port. USB ports are faster, and each port can support many devices connected in series. USBs can accommodate printers, CD-ROM devices, and even modems. A few devices—in particular, the modem—still use serial ports. The vast majority of modems connect to the serial port, so you'll need to know how to troubleshoot these ports and make them work with modems.

Serial Port Settings

The characteristics of a serial port are as follows:

Baud rate   The speed at which data moves on the serial cable in bits per second.

Data bits   The number of bits of data in a byte (either 7 or 8 bits per byte).

Parity   A special bit that determines whether the correct number of bits have been transmitted. The parity setting can be even, odd, space, mark, or none.

Stop bits   Two bits that determine the beginning and end of a byte.

The computer and the device connected to the serial port must have the same settings, or they will not be able to communicate. The flow of data over a serial cable is regulated by one of two methods:

- RTS/CTS (Request To Send/Clear To Send), also called *hardware flow control,* uses two wires to signal the CPU that the device is ready to accept data (Clear To Send, CTS) or send data (Request To Send, RTS).

- XON/XOFF, also called *software flow control,* uses two special characters to stop and restart the transmission of data. When the buffer is filled, it sends the XOFF character. When the CPU (or the device) has processed the data in the buffer and is ready to accept more data, it sends the XON character to resume transmission.

Handshaking

Two serial ports communicate through a well-defined process known as *handshaking.* One of the devices involved in the handshaking process, the computer, is the Data Terminal Equipment (DTE). The other device, the peripheral device, is the Data Communications Equipment (DCE). Here's the outline of the handshaking process:

1. The DTE turns on the DTR (Data Transmit Ready) wire.

2. The DCE turns on the DSR (Data Set Ready) wire. Both devices are now ready to communicate.

3. The DTE turns on the RTS (Request To Send) wire, which tells the DCE that it's ready to send data.

4. If the DCE is ready, it acknowledges the request by turning on the CTS (Clear To Send) wire.

5. The two devices can now exchange data. DTE transmits on the TD line (Transmit Data on pin 2), while the DCE transmits on the RD line (Receive Data on pin 3). When the DCE needs to stop the transmission, it puts a signal on either the RTS or the CTS wire. Transmission resumes when the device is ready to accept more data and it signals the RTS or CTS wire.

Physical and Logical Serial Ports

All computers have two serial ports, named COM1 and COM2. These ports are assigned specific *interrupts* (special signal lines assigned to devices for communicating with the CPU). When the COM1 port needs the CPU's attention, it raises the interrupt 4 (IRQ 4), which maps to the I/O address 3F8h. In the same manner, the COM2 port uses the interrupt 3, which maps to the I/O address 2F8h. The interrupts request the CPU's attention, and the specific I/O address is used by both devices to talk to each other.

COM1 and COM2 are the physical ports of the computer. Because of the variety of devices that can be connected to serial ports, designers created a technique that allows multiple devices to be connected to the same physical port. Additional serial devices can be connected to logical ports, which are COM3 and COM4. COM3 is a logical port that uses the same interrupt and I/O address as COM1; and COM4 is a logical port that uses the same interrupt and I/O address as COM2. Even though you can have multiple devices connected to the same physical port, the software will distinguish between them.

Serial ports can't be daisy-chained like USB and SCSI ports. So how do we connect two devices on the same port? You can connect only one device to each serial port on the back of the computer. But there are expansion cards that use the logical ports. An internal modem, for example, can be assigned to the COM3 port. A multifunction expansion card can take up the COM4 port and provide a third serial port, where you can connect another external device. In the past, serial devices were quite common (many printers were designed as serial devices), but the importance of the serial port is declining. Nowadays, only modems and pointing devices are connected to serial ports.

Types of Serial Cables

Any device that connects to a serial port comes with its own cable. If the number of pins on the computer's end doesn't match the number of pins on the device's serial port, you can buy a 9-pin-to-25-pin (or 25-pin-to-9-pin) serial cable adapter at any computer store.

All computers now come with one or two (usually two) 9-pin serial ports. Some devices, however, may require a so-called *null modem*; this is a cable that connects the serial ports on two similar devices, such as two DTE or two DCE devices. If you need to connect two computers over their serial ports, for example, you'll need a null modem cable. The wire diagrams of various null modem cables are shown in Chapter 21 of *The Complete PC Upgrade & Maintenance Guide* (see the section "Common Cables: A Configuration Cookbook").

Of course, any serial-port-to-serial-port connection will work only if the two serial ports have the same settings.

To exchange files between two computers, you must use a utility specifically designed for this purpose. One is the HyperTerminal utility supplied with Windows 95/98; it's discussed in the Exercise section of this chapter. Most such utilities move data through the parallel port, because it's much faster than the serial port. You can actually connect two Windows 95/98 machines with a parallel port and establish a two-computer network. Each computer can see the other computer's hard drives and printer and thus can share the resources. This type of network is very handy when you have to back up a user's files before you start working on the hard drives. You can connect your notebook to the other computer's parallel port, copy all data files to your notebook, and then repair the other computer. If you have to format the disk, you can reinstall the operating system and applications and then move the data from your notebook back to the fixed computer.

The Parallel Port

The parallel port is much simpler than the serial port, and you'll never have to configure a parallel port. Unlike the serial port, the parallel port works asynchronously and transfers data much faster, because it moves one byte at a time. You should be aware of the three types of parallel ports in use today:

- The Standard Parallel Port (SPP), which moves data from the computer to the printer, but not in the other direction. This is the oldest type of parallel port.

- The Enhanced Parallel Port (EPP), which allows data to be moved in both directions. This type of port allows printers to send information back to the computer.

- The Enhanced Capabilities Port (ECP), which allows bidirectional flow of information. These ports are ideal for connecting external backup devices.

Parallel Port Daisy-Chaining

Many devices you connect to the ECP provide a printer cable connector, so that you can daisy-chain two devices on the same parallel port. To connect an external Zip drive to the computer, you attach it to the parallel port of the computer. Then you can connect the printer to the second port on the Zip drive with another parallel cable. Note that this is not a function of the parallel port. When you connect an Iomega Zip drive to the computer's parallel port and then the printer to the drive, it's the drive's hardware and software that manage the two devices on the same port. When the computer sends data to the printer, the drive passes them to the printer's connector. When you're accessing the Zip disk, the information is blocked by the drive and the printer never sees it.

Exercise

To Configure Serial Ports

To set the connection properties of the COM1 serial port, you can use the following DOS command:

```
MODE COM1: BAUD=9600 PARITY=odd DATA=8 STOP=1
```

To set the connection properties of a COM port under Windows 95/98, use the following steps:

1. Start the Device Manager: Open the Start menu and select Settings ➢ Control Panel ➢ System. When the System Properties menu appears, select the Device Manager tab.

2. A list of all devices on your computer is displayed. Click the plus sign in front of the item Ports (COM & LPT), and you'll see all the serial and parallel ports on your computer.

3. Select the COM1 item (or the name of the serial port you want to configure) and click the Properties button on the tab.

4. In the Communications Port Properties, select the Port Settings tab. On this tab you can see the port's connection characteristics and change their values.

Accessing the Parallel Port

This test bypasses all the Windows drivers of the serial port. If it works, you'll know that the printer is operational and the link is working between the computer and the printer.

Test the parallel port and printer by sending a few lines of text to the printer with the following DOS command:

```
COPY CON LPT1

Parallel printer test

This is the second test line

End Of Test

^Z
```

Note that the last line is a Ctrl+Z character, which must appear at the beginning of a new line and must be followed by a Return.

A few seconds later, the three text lines should be printed on a new page.

To Communicate with a Serial Device

This procedure shows you how to communicate with a device on the serial or parallel port, using the HyperTerminal program.

1. Click the Start button and select Programs ➢ Accessories ➢ Communications ➢ HyperTerminal.

2. When the HyperTerminal folder appears, double-click the Hypertrm icon.

3. In the Connection Properties dialog box, enter the name of the new connection (name it **Serial**) and click OK.

4. Next you'll see the Connect To dialog box. In the Connect Using box, select the name of the port to which the modem is connected. The appropriate Properties dialog box appears.

5. You can set the properties of the serial port at will, since the modem will adjust automatically to the settings of the serial port.

6. Click the OK button, and a terminal window appears. Here you can enter commands to be sent to the modem and see the modem's response.

7. Enter the **AT** command and press Enter. The modem should reply with the string OK. Consult your modem's manual to find out what other commands you can send to the modem.

To Connect Two Computers Over the Parallel Port

Windows 95/98 allows you network two computers with a parallel cable. This is a very handy feature when you need to back up a lot of data files at a client's side and no backup devices are available. When you upgrade the operating system on a computer with a single drive, or when a computer doesn't have enough space to back up the master drive, you can create a mirror of the master disk on another computer's disk.

Following is the process for networking two computers through their parallel ports. Before you begin, you must buy a parallel cable and connect the parallel ports on the two computers. Then you can take these steps to set up the two computers.

To Set Up Computer A

1. Click the Start button and select Programs ➤ Accessories ➤ Communications ➤ Direct Cable Connection to invoke the Direct Cable Connection utility.

2. When the first dialog box appears, you're prompted to specify whether the computer will be the host or the guest. Set Computer A as the host. Computer A will monitor its parallel port for a request by the guest computer. If you have established a direct cable connection in the past, you'll see another window that displays the role of the computer (host or guest). Click the Change button to change the computer's role.

3. Click the Next button to proceed. In the next dialog box, select the port you're using to connect. For this exercise, select Parallel Port on LPT1. As you can see, it's possible to connect two computers via the serial port, too, but this connection is considerably slower. You can also network two computers via the infrared port, if one is available.

4. Click the Next button. You're prompted to enter a password. Although it's not really needed, check the box in the window and click the Set Password button. Specify the password and click Finish.

5. The following message appears, indicating that the host computer is waiting for the guest computer to connect:

   `Status: Waiting to connect via Parallel cable on LPT1.`

   At this point, Computer A is waiting for Computer B to connect. Switch to Computer B and continue with the steps in the next section.

To Set Up Computer B

6. Click the Start button and select Programs ➤ Accessories ➤ Communications ➤ Direct Cable Connection to invoke the Direct Cable Connection utility.

7. When the first dialog box appears, you're prompted to specify whether the computer will be the host or the guest. Set Computer B as the guest. Computer B will attempt to connect to the host computer through the parallel port. If you have previously established a direct cable connection, you'll see another window that displays the role of the computer (host or guest). Click the Change button to change the computer's role.

8. Click the Connect button, and you'll see the following message:

   `Connecting via Parallel Cable on LPTn`

   where n is the number of the parallel port. This message should disappear quickly and you'll be prompted to enter the password you specified in the host computer. Enter the password and click OK.

Once you have established communication between the two computers, you must share the drive of one of the computers, or the drives on both computers. To do so, right-click the drive and select Properties; in the Properties dialog box of the selected drive, switch to the Sharing tab. On the Sharing tab check the option Shared As. You can name the share and, optionally, set a password. If one of the computers has a printer and you want to be able to use from the other computer, you'll have to share it as well.

From now on you'll be able to access the hard drive of the host computer as if it were a local drive, as well as all the shared resources of the host computer.

Lab 26

DATE _____ NAME _____

1. What's the difference between serial and parallel ports?

_____

_____

_____

_____

_____

2. Describe the process of handshaking.

_____

_____

_____

_____

_____

_____

_____

_____

_____

3. Is there a handshaking process for parallel ports, and why?

_____

_____

_____

4. What are the characteristics of a serial connection between a computer and a modem or another serial device?

_____

_____

_____

_____

_____

_____

Lab 27: Installing a Modem

Objectives for This Lab

Upon completion of this lab, you will be able to

1. Install an internal modem.

2. Troubleshoot common hardware-related modem problems.

Hardware & Software Requirements

Hardware:

1. A working PC computer

2. A modem

3. A Phillips screwdriver

4. An antistatic wrist strap

Software: Any installation software that comes with the modem

What to Read in the Book

Chapter 3, pages 217–18; Chapter 21, page 888–89; Chapter 31, pages 1287–88, The Complete PC Upgrade & Maintenance Guide, Mark Minasi, Sybex

Introduction

A few years ago, people bought external modems for two primary reasons: If you bought a new computer, you could easily transfer the modem to the new machine, and you could easily use the modem on the road with a laptop. Today, modem prices are very low and almost all portables include a built-in modem; therefore, few external modems are used. But if you do have one, installation instructions are simple: Plug it into the serial port on the outside of your computer. In this lab, we'll describe the process of installing the much more common *internal* modem—as well as how to get the operating system to work with that modem.

A modem translates (*mo*dulates) digital information streaming out of the computer into a series of audible squawks and beeps. (You hear this noise after the modem starts communicating with another modem, but once the connection is made, the speaker in the modem is programmed to shut itself down.) Phone lines are designed to carry audio information (your voice), so the computer's digital data must be modulated into audio noises. The modem on the other end of the phone call *dem*odulates (translates the audio back into digital data). *M*odulates and *dem*odulates = Modem. Get it?

An internal modem (like an external modem) attaches to the computer's serial port. However, the internal modem goes into a card slot on the motherboard, whereas an external modem is connected to the computer via a DB9 to DB25 cable. The exception is the USB (Universal Serial Bus) connection. Most mice attach to the serial port, too.

By far the most common serial ports used are COM1 (typically used for the mouse) and COM2 (typically used for the modem). The specifications for a standard PC computer include theoretical COM3 and COM4 ports, but they are rarely used.

NOTE   Having only two really functional serial ports (ports 3 and 4 are, alas, not very useful for technical reasons) can cause a traffic problem. Too many devices can compete for these two working ports: handheld devices such as the PalmPilot, some kinds of scanners, digital cameras, even some printers contend with modems and mice for these two precious portals. The solution to this problem is the USB port.

Exercise

To Install an Internal Modem

1. Turn off the computer, unplug all external cables, and open the case.

2. Locate an empty PCI slot (the smallest slot type).

3. Unscrew the screw that holds the small metal plate on the back of the case, behind the PCI slot.

4. Carefully insert the modem into the slot.

5. Screw the tab at the end of the modem into the computer case.

6. Plug the phone cord into the modem's Line In plug.

7. Insert the floppy diskette or CD that came with the modem and run the modem's setup program to install its drivers or other software. If you're using an operating system with Plug and Play (Windows 98, NT 4, or Windows 2000), simply turn on the computer's power and wait for the operating system to detect the new device and, if necessary, ask for the diskette or CD that holds the driver.

To Solve Common Modem Hardware Problems

If you're having difficulty getting a new modem to respond to your efforts to dial out, try these steps to cure the problem:

1. Ensure that the phone line is plugged into the modem. Usually, the phone line from the outside is plugged into one receptacle on the back of the modem, and then a second phone line connects a second receptacle on the back of the modem to the telephone.

2. Make sure that the modem is plugged into the computer. An internal modem should be well seated in the slot; for an external modem, the serial cable should be securely attached to both the modem and the computer's serial port connector.

3. Confirm that the outside line is live by plugging the outside phone line into the telephone to see if you get a dial tone.

4. Remember that you must use special, additional dial commands to get an outside line if you work in an office that has a special in-house telephone system (such as ROLM).

NOTE   For details on establishing a dial-up connection to the Internet in Windows and using the Internet Connection Wizard, see Lab 28.

Lab 27

DATE _____ NAME _____

1. Which are more popular today: external or internal modems? Why?

_____

_____

_____

2. Which port is typically used for the modem, and which for the mouse?

_____

_____

_____

3. After you've physically attached a modem to the computer, what steps do you take next to install the modem's software (driver)?

_____

_____

_____

_____

4. Describe two common modem hardware problems and their solutions.

_____

_____

_____

Lab 28: Connecting to the Internet

Objectives for This Lab

Upon completion of this lab, you will be able to

1. Understand and gather the information needed to establish a dial-up connection to the Internet in Windows.

2. Use the Internet Connection Wizard to define a dial-up connection to your ISP (Internet Service Provider).

Hardware & Software Requirements

Hardware:

1. A working PC computer

2. A modem or other physical connection to the Internet

Software: Internet Explorer, Netscape Navigator, or other communications software

What to Read in the Book

Chapter 30, pages 1233–36, *The Complete PC Upgrade & Maintenance Guide*, Mark Minasi, Sybex

Introduction

Lab 4 of this manual states that the Internet is an essential source of information for PC technicians or anyone responsible for maintaining a computer. Larger companies that need continuous Internet service typically have dedicated T-1 or T-3 connections, but many individuals and smaller shops use a *dial-up connection*—using ordinary telephone lines to connect through an ISP. Increasingly popular, though, are high-speed, always-on ISDN (Integrated Services Digital Network) telephone line connections, and cable modem connections.

Fortunately, today you can get connected to the Internet without having to go through too much setup and installation grief. Operating systems such as Windows 95/98, NT, and Windows 2000 take you step-by-step through the process using their Internet Connection Wizard—utility software that asks a set of questions and then automatically stores the information necessary to create the dial-up connection.

Dial-Up Connections

Before creating a dial-up connection, let's consider what happens when your machine talks to another machine over the Internet. Data is divided into *packets* and then sent over the Internet using *protocols* (sets of rules). TCP (the Transmission Control Protocol) ensures that all the data arrives at its target, and that the packets of data arrive in the correct order. IP (the Internet Protocol) works in concert with TCP, but the IP's job is to actually transport the data from your modem to a target modem's address. These two protocols are always referred to as a single entity, TCP/IP. Working with TCP/IP is the PPP (Point-to-Point Protocol), which makes the Internet see your machine as having a valid IP address so you can directly receive data.

You purchase time on the Internet from an ISP—telephone giant AT&T is an ISP, as are Microsoft, AOL (America Online), and hundreds of others. Your local newspaper probably offers an Internet connection, as do other, usually small, local servers. You can purchase Internet time by the hour or in other time packages, including unlimited use for around $20 per month.

From your ISP you get a few pieces of essential information that you must supply to the Internet Connection Wizard so it can set up a dial-up connection for you. You'll see this information listed in this lab's Exercise section.

New Shared Internet Connections in Windows 2000

Windows 2000 users can exploit a new *shared connections* feature: People on a network (even a humble home network) can share the same dial-up connection. After you've established a dial-up connection using the My Network Places icon on your desktop, right-click the new connection's icon and select Properties. Click the Sharing tab, and select the option to enable Internet connection sharing for this connection.

If you use a LAN, both Windows 98 and 2000 can detect shared Internet connections or proxy servers automatically. To set this up, run Internet Explorer and choose Tools ➤ Internet Options. Click the Connections tab, then the LAN Settings button, and select the Automatically Detect Settings check box.

ISDN and Cable Service

For the past few years, it's been possible to speed up your connection to the Internet by installing an ISDN connection to replace the usual phone-line connection. This usually costs a fair amount of money, but you can communicate about four times faster than the average Internet connection. Today, though, satellite TV, cable TV, and others are rushing to offer far faster connections at a far lower cost than ISDN. For about $40 per month, you get the following advantages with a typical cable TV-based Internet connection:

- It's always on, just like TV—no need to dial a connection or use up a phone line.
- It's fast. A cable TV connection is about 124 times as fast as a 28.8KB modem connection, and about 7.5 times as fast as an ISDN connection.

But there's a hidden "gotcha" for those who travel: You can't drag your cable with you. If you need to get e-mail on the road, you'll also have to maintain a traditional ISP that you can call over the phone by using your portable. However, cable modem suppliers such as Time-Warner's RoadRunner are promising to solve the mobility problem in the future. Perhaps they'll offer an 800 number and charge a nominal fee such as ten cents a minute.

Keep in mind that ISDN and cable connections are more vulnerable to intrusion by hackers than traditional modem connections. For a good solution to this problem, see the "Safety First" sidebar.

Safety First: Protecting Yourself from Internet Invasions

One of the problems with an always-on cable or ISDN connection is that you get assigned a permanent Internet address. As a result, you're vulnerable to hackers who send automated programs roaming the Internet, trying out addresses at random, looking for weaknesses in their protection. Like a thief who wanders through parking lots looking for cars with a key in the ignition, a roaming "spider" searches for an open connection. When one is found, the spider reports back to its hacker owner, who can then come back to that address at any time to see what files are of interest, or to do damage.

You can protect yourself from this threat with an excellent product called ZoneAlarm. Free to individual personal computer users, and $19.95 per seat for business, government, or education customers, ZoneAlarm is a popular solution for those concerned about possible hack-attacks. It works on Windows 95, 98, NT 4.0, or Windows 2000 (if you've been beta testing, use only the Final Release version of Windows 2000).

ZoneAlarm is a software-based firewall that can stand firmly between your quivering, vulnerable little hard drive and the big, bad World Wide Web with its roving, hideous hairy hacker spiders. Follow these steps to install ZoneAlarm:

1. Type this address into your browser:

   ```
   hotfiles.zdnet.com/cgi-bin/texis/swlib/hotfiles/
       info.html?fcode=0015P7&b=lod
   ```

   If you find this address is no longer available, go to one of the following:

   ```
   www.zdnet.com/special/filters/defense/action
   www.zdnet.com
   ```

   or just use a search engine like Google to search for Shields Up!, ZoneAlarm's home page.

2. Click the Download Now button to start the download of ZoneAlarm. When asked, choose to save the file to your hard drive. The entire file should take less than a minute to download.

3. Locate the Zonalarm.exe file on your hard drive and double-click it to install.

4. Click Next several times to complete the steps for installation.

Exercise

To Connect to the Internet in Windows or NT

1. Make an agreement to purchase time on the Internet from an ISP.

2. To verify that your version of Windows has the dial-up networking feature installed, double-click the Add/Remove Programs icon in Control Panel. Then click the Windows Setup tab in the Add/Remove Programs Properties dialog box that comes up. Next, click the Communications option in the list box and click the Details button. If the check box next to Dial-up Networking is checked, dial-up networking is already installed on your machine. If it isn't, click the check box, click the OK button, and follow the instructions to install dial-up networking from your Windows CD.

3. In Control Panel, click the Internet Options icon.

4. In the Internet Properties dialog box, click the Connections tab.

5. Click the Setup button to bring up the Internet Connection Wizard.

6. Choose the I Want to Transfer My Existing Internet Account to This Computer option. (This assumes you've contacted an ISP in step 1.)

7. Click the Next button and follow the Wizard's instructions, answering all its questions with the information that was supplied by your ISP. Precisely what's required in this step depends on your ISP, so some of the following information may not be necessary:

   - The local phone number to dial to get a connection to the ISP's server

   - Your username (sometimes called your account name)

   - Your logon password

   - Your e-mail address

   - Your e-mail password

   - Your primary DNS (Domain Name System) server (a set of four numbers separated by periods—for example, 208.243.52.175)

   - Your secondary DNS server (another "dotted quad" number), if your ISP has provided one

   - Your POP (Point of Presence, or general) server name

   - Your SMTP (Simple Mail Transfer Protocol, or e-mail) server name

   - Your NNTP (Network News Transfer Protocol, or newsgroup) server name

Troubleshooting the Internet Connection Wizard

If your dial-up connection doesn't work, first double-check the information you entered via the Wizard by following these steps:

1. In Control Panel, double-click the Internet Options icon.

2. In the Internet Properties dialog box, click the Connections tab. Select your ISP connection in the list box titled Dial-up Settings, and then click the Settings button.

3. In the Connection to *ConnectionName* Settings dialog box that appears, check your username and retype your logon password (*not* your e-mail password).

4. Click the Properties button and make sure the telephone number is correct.

5. Then click the Server Types tab, click the TCP/IP Settings button, and check your primary and secondary DNS numbers.

Lab 28

DATE _____ NAME _____

1. What is a dial-up connection, and how do you create one?

_____

_____

_____

_____

_____

_____

_____

_____

2. Describe the advantages and disadvantages of an ISDN or cable-modem Internet connection.

_____

_____

_____

_____

_____

_____

_____

3. There are ten pieces of information that most ISPs must give you before you can create a dial-up connection. Name five of them.

_____

_____

_____

_____

_____

_____

4. What should you do first if your dial-up connection doesn't work?

_____

_____

_____

_____

Lab 29: Networking PCs

Objectives for This Lab

Upon completion of this lab, you will be able to

1. Install and configure network cards.

2. Connect PCs to a network.

Hardware & Software Requirements

Hardware:

1. A working PC computer

2. A Network Interface Card (NIC)

3. An antistatic wrist strap

4. A Phillips screwdriver

Software:

1. The installation CD or floppies that came with the NIC

2. The Windows installation CD

What to Read in the Book

Chapter 27, *The Complete PC Upgrade & Maintenance Guide*, Mark Minasi, Sybex

Introduction

Even the smallest companies nowadays network their computers. The advantages of networking computers are discussed in detail in the book, so here we'll review the basic ingredients of a local computer network, which are the computers (obviously), the network interface cards, and the cables that connect the computers to each other. Setting up the hardware isn't adequate to create a network; you'll need to install the appropriate software, but this software comes with Windows.

NOTE   A company that deploys a LAN should assign a person to administer the resources of the LAN—to decide which drives will be shared, connect printers to the network, set user privileges for the users, and so on. Of course, small companies with just a few users can't justify the cost of a network administrator, so they'll pass the responsibility of maintaining the network to a programmer or to the most experienced user. As a hardware person, you should be able to fix minor network problems, add new workstations to the network and, in general, perform basic network troubleshooting. Although it's not typically your responsibility to set up and troubleshoot LANs, you will inevitably be called to resolve network problems. Obviously, we can't teach networking concepts in a single lab. The goal here is to familiarize you with the basic ingredients of a network, the way the computers are connected to each other, and the software components that enable the networked computers to converse.

Network Hardware

The basic component of a LAN is the Network Interface Card (NIC), which must exist in every networked PC. The most common NICs today operate at speeds of 100MBps. Older NICs operated at 10MBps, and many LANs deploy NICs operating at both speeds (known as 10/100 NICs). If you have to replacing an existing NIC, make sure it operates at 100MBps.

Each NIC is equipped with a connector, where you hook the cables that connect the PC to the rest of the network. Most NICs today are equipped with an RJ-45 connector and/or a BNC connector. The RJ-45 connector looks like the jack you use to hook your phone to the line, only it's thicker. The RJ-45 connectors are used for a cable that's the same as the one used by the telephones, the twisted pair. There are two variations of twisted-pair cables, the unshielded twisted pair (UTP) and the shielded twisted pair (STP). UTP contains four pairs of wires and STP contains two pairs of wires. You'll find pictures of all the connectors (on the cables and on the NIC) in Chapter 27 of *The Complete PC Maintenance & Upgrade Guide*.

BNC is a round connector for coaxial cables. The coaxial cable is thick and relatively flexible, but not nearly as flexible as the twisted pair. Its bandwidth is lower than that of the twisted pair, 10 megabits per second (Mbps), but it runs longer distances. The twisted pair operates at 100Mbps, but it can't carry the signal for more than 100 meters without amplification. Table 27.1 in *The Complete PC Maintenance & Upgrade Guide* summarizes the cable types, the maximum distances they cover, and the maximum speed at which they can operate.

If the network uses coaxial cable, you need a T connector to plug the cable into the NIC. The T connector is shaped like a T, with the base on the card. On the other two ends of the connector you connect two cables, each one to a different computer. The computers on this LAN are connected in series; if one segment is broken, the network breaks. The computers at the two ends of the cable have only an incoming cable. The other end of the T connector must be capped with a terminator, a small device that is screwed on the connection and has a built-in resistor that prevents the echoing of the signal.

If the network uses twisted pair, then all computers are connected to a central device: the hub. (In many older installations, there's no hub. Instead, all cables end up at a patch panel in a wiring closet. But you can't build a TCP/IP network without hubs.) The hub interconnects a number of computers; hubs are available for 2, 4, 8, 16, and even more computers. You can also connect two hubs to each other to add more workstations. For larger installations, you'll need a hub switch to interconnect multiple hubs. If the LAN runs over several floors, you'll need one hub for each floor, and a hub switch that will connect all the hubs to each other. Hubs are intelligent enough not to transmit to the rest of the network the packets that are exchanged between two computers connected to the same hub. Finally, if you run out of connectors on the hub, you can connect one or two computers directly to the hub switch.

TIP   The cabling of the network must be designed by a professional. It's important to lay out a structured network so that you can add new workstations over time without having to rearrange the existing computers.

Network Software

In addition to the hardware for a network, you need to install certain software to make the connected computers see each other. Installing network software can get quite complicated. And just about any user can network a few Windows computers. Most users will install drivers and protocols until they get each computer to see the rest of them. But these networks are inefficient and difficult to manage. So if you're called to install a new network, you'll find the information in this chapter to be inadequate. The topic of networking computers is far too vast to be covered in a single chapter. Here we'll simply help you figure out how the computers are interconnected, what protocols they use, and how to replace a NIC or add a new one to a computer. As you work on through the network installation, don't be embarrassed to say "I don't know" or to ask for help from the vendor supplying the networking hardware.

When you install a network with Windows, you'll install the following items. All the necessary actions can be performed through the Network Properties dialog box (right-click the Network Neighborhood icon and select Properties from the shortcut menu).

Adapter   This is the NIC that connects each computer to the others in the network.

Protocol   This is the language through which your computer talks to the other networked computers. Notice that you can have multiple protocols on the same network. The most common protocol is TCP/IP, but NetBEUI and Novell's IPX/SPX are also quite common. All computers on the network must use the same protocol, so that they can talk to each other. You may have Windows machines and one or more NetWare servers on the same network, for instance—not at all an unusual situation. In this case, you'll have to install the TCP/IP protocol so that the Windows machines can converse, as well as the IPX/SPX protocol so that the same machines can see the NetWare server. The applications will use the proper protocol, depending on the operation.

Client This is the software that enables a computer to connect to the other networked computers. If you want to connect to other Windows machines, you must add the Client for Microsoft Networks.

Service You must add a service that tells the computer how to function on the network. The Microsoft File and Printer Sharing service, for example, allows a user to share resources such as disks and printers on one computer with others on the network, as well as to access the shared resources on the other computers. An indication of a poorly designed network is that *all* resources are shared and any user can access any resource without a password. This is especially dangerous if one of the computers has access to the Internet.

Exercise

To Document the Existing Network Configuration

1. Examine the cable coming out of a computer's NIC. Write down its type (BNC, Shielded/Unshielded Twisted Pair).

2. Create a diagram of the LAN you're using. Draw a box for each computer and use straight lines to draw the cables that connect the computers. Be sure to include the hubs or hub switches that are used in the LAN.

3. Right-click the Network Neighborhood icon on the desktop and select Properties. In the Network dialog box that appears, you can see the list of all the components installed on the computer. Write down the components and their settings. To view each component's settings, select the component in the Network dialog box and click the Properties button.

To Install a New NIC

In this procedure, you'll learn how to install a new (or replace an existing) Network Interface Card (NIC). You shouldn't attempt to set up a network from scratch—that is the network administrator's job. Nevertheless, you should be able to add a new computer to the network by installing a new card and plugging in the necessary cables.

1. Turn off the computer, unplug all the cables, and open the case. As in earlier labs, don't forget your antistatic wrist strap.

2. If the computer doesn't have a NIC installed, go to step 3. If you're replacing an existing NIC, remove the screw that holds the card on the chassis and remove the card. Do not attempt to remove the card while it's connected to the cable.

3. Set the jumpers on the card. Most newer cards don't have switches; instead, you set their IRQ through the Setup software that comes with the card. Then insert the card into the same slot. If the new card is a type that's different from the old one (say you're replacing an ISA card with a PCI card), you'll use a different slot, of course. Also, some PCI computers require that you enable the PCI slots through the BIOS Setup program before using them. Close the computer when you're ready.

4. Plug in all the cables, connect the NIC to the network cable, and turn the computer on. If the new network card has LEDs, watch them as the computer starts up. Read the card's manual to see if the proper LEDs have come on. A green blinking LED usually indicates that the card can see the network—although this doesn't mean that the computer can talk to other computers on the network.

5. Most network cards operate at both 10MBps and 100MBps. The current speed of the card is indicated by an LED. Consult the documentation and make sure the card is operating at the desired speed. Most 10/100 cards will sense the speed of the hub they're connected to and adjust their own speed.

6. At this point, Windows should detect the new card and install the new drivers. If the card isn't Plug and Play, you'll have to insert the CD or floppies that came with the card and install it manually. Consult the documentation to find out which program (usually a SETUP.EXE or INSTALL.EXE file) you must execute to install the card.

7. After running the card's Setup program, run the diagnostics. The software that comes with the card includes some diagnostic software that will verify the correct installation of the card.

8. Now right-click the Network Neighborhood icon and select Properties to get the Network dialog box. If this NIC is replacing an existing one, Windows will adjust all the settings in this dialog box and you may not have to do anything. If the card wasn't Plug and Play, however, you'll have to add the necessary components manually.

9. Remove all the services, protocols, clients, and the network adapter, to install everything from scratch. During this process, Windows may prompt you to restart the computer for the changes to take effect, but do not restart the computer until you've implemented all the changes (you'll restart the computer later at step 15).

10. Next, you add the drivers for the network adapter (the card you just installed). Even if Windows has a driver for this card, you should connect to the Web site of the card's manufacturer and

download the latest drivers. When you're prompted to select the card's maker and model, click Have Disk to install the newer drivers.

11. Once the adapter has been installed, click the Add button and this time select Protocol. In the list of protocols, choose Microsoft; then from the Microsoft protocols select the one that's used by the other computers on the network. You'll most likely install the TCP/IP and NetBEUI protocols.

12. After installing the necessary protocols, Windows will bind them automatically to the network card. The binding means that Windows will use the TCP/IP protocol (or any protocol you've installed) to communicate with the other computers through the network card you just installed. It's possible for a computer to have two network cards, each one bound to a different protocol.

13. When you return to the Network dialog box, click the Add button again and this time select Client. Then select the same client as the other computers use. Here you will most likely select the Client for Microsoft Networks. If there are Novell servers on the network, you will also select the Client for NetWare Networks.

14. The last step is the installation of the File and Printer Sharing for Microsoft Networks service. With this service you'll be able to access the shared resources of other computers on the network.

15. When you're prompted to restart the computer so that the changes take effect, do so. When the computer restarts, you should be able to see the network. If not, start the Troubleshooter and follow the steps. Connecting a computer to the network shouldn't be a hassle, but it's not simple.

16. The last step is to decide which of the computer's resources you want to share with other users. (If you're replacing an existing network card, the proper resources on the computer are already shared.) To make a resource available to other users, right-click the resource (a drive, printer, or other peripheral) and select Properties. In the Properties dialog box Sharing tab, specify that the resource will be shared. You can also set a password, so that only selected users can access the share. If the workstation is using Windows NT or Windows 2000, ask the network administrator to set the appropriate shares and permissions.

Installing a TCP/IP Network

Follow these steps to install the TCP/IP protocol on a small number of networked computers. We're assuming you have installed a network interface card on every machine and connected them to each other. The procedure shown here must be repeated for all computers on the network.

1. Right-click the Network Neighborhood icon and select Properties. In the Network dialog box, select Add and then Protocol. In the Select Network Protocol dialog box that appears, choose Microsoft in the list of manufacturers, and choose TCP/IP in the list of available protocols.

2. As soon as you specify the new protocol, Windows will bind it to all adapters. Most likely, each computer has two adapters: the NIC and the dial-up adapter (which is the modem).

3. When you return to the Network dialog box, select the line TCP/IP -> *NIC* (where *NIC* is the name of the adapter you have installed) and click the Properties button. Here you're going to set the properties of TCP/IP on the NIC.

4. On the IP Address tab, check the option Specify an IP Address; in the IP Address box below, enter an address. Use the format **198.162.0.XXX**, where **XXX** is a number in the range 0 to 255 and is different for every machine on the network.

5. Click the DNS Configuration tab to open it, and disable DNS. Then open the WINS tab and disable WINS Resolution. Click OK to return to the Network dialog box.

6. Click the Add button again and this time select Client. In the Select Network Client dialog box, choose Microsoft in the Manufacturer list and choose Client for Microsoft Networks in the Network Clients list. Then click OK.

7. In the Network dialog box, click Add once more. This time select a Service; choose the File and Printer Sharing for Microsoft Networks service.

8. If all computers have a different IP address, you can share selected resources on each computer. Select the hard drives, printers, and CD-ROM drive you want to share among the network users. Then right-click each resource and select Sharing.

9. In the Sharing tab of the Properties dialog box, check the Shared As option and enter a name for the share. Under Windows 98 you can set a password for the share, so that only users who know the password can access the shared resource. Under Windows NT/2000 you can assign specific privileges on the share for various users or groups of users.

onnecting to a NetWare Server

ne network contains a NetWare server, follow these steps to give the users of the Windows hines access to the NetWare server.

Add the protocol IPX/SPX Compatible Protocol from Microsoft. This protocol will bind automatically to the network card. (Notice that the IPX/SPX protocol will also bind to the dial-up adapter. You can remove this binding by selecting it with the mouse and clicking the Remove button.)

Click the Add button to add a new client: Client for NetWare Networks.

3. When you return to the Client dialog box, select the new client (Client for NetWare Networks) and click Properties. In the dialog box that appears, open the General tab. Enter the name of the NetWare server you want to access. (You can also set a letter name for the server's first drive. The other drives will be named with the subsequent letters.)

4. Add a new service: File and Printer Sharing for NetWare Networks.

5. Click OK to close the Network dialog box. Windows displays a message box telling you that you must restart the computer for the changes to take effect.

Sharing an Internet Connection

Another good reason for networking multiple computers is to give them access to the Internet through a single modem. If you install an ISDN line (or an even faster connection to the Internet), you can configure all computers on the LAN to access the Internet through a single computer (as opposed to installing multiple modems and sharing telephone lines).

To access the Internet through a single computer, you must install the Internet Connection Sharing utility, which comes with Windows 98SE.

1. First, install the Internet Connection Sharing component through the Add/Remove Programs utility of the Control Panel. Select the Windows Setup tab. Look for the Internet Connection Sharing utility under the Internet Tools group.

2. The installation program will assign a number to the computer that serves as the gateway to th Internet. This number is 198.162.0.0. The addresses in this class can only be used internally o a LAN. They will not cause any conflicts with other computers on the Internet, because all addresses of the form 198.162.0.XXX are internal to a LAN and can't be reached from outsi the network. The group of digits represented by XXX is in the range 0 to 255, for a total of 25 possible local addresses.

3. The installation program will create a diskette with the drivers you must install on the oth computers.

4. Take the diskette and install the software on the other computers. Each time you install the ware, that computer will be assigned the next IP address. For example, the first client comp takes the address 198.162.0.1, the next client takes 198.162.0.2, and so on. This inform is stored on the diskette, so you must use the same diskette to install the drivers for shar Internet connection on all workstations on the network.

Lab 29

DATE _____ NAME _____

1. When would you use a hub to interconnect several computers, and when is a hub switch necessary?

_____

_____

_____

_____

_____

2. What are the resources you can share on your computer?

_____

_____

_____

_____

_____

3. Write down the adapter, the protocol, and the service and client names in use on the network. Why do some networks require more than one protocol?

_____

_____

_____

_____

_____

Lab 30: Installing a Sound Card

Objectives for This Lab

Upon completion of this lab, you will be able to

1. Put a sound card into your computer.

2. Connect the card to external speakers and a CD or DVD player.

3. Troubleshoot the physical installation of the sound card.

Hardware & Software Requirements

Hardware:

1. A working PC computer

2. A sound card

3. A Phillips screwdriver

4. An antistatic wrist strap

ftware:

1. The CD that came with the sound card, containing drivers for the card

2. Utility software

hat to Read in the Book

ter 24; Chapter 32, page 1336, *The Complete PC Upgrade & Maintenance Guide*, Mark Minasi,

duction

sical installation of a sound card is usually fairly straightforward. It's much the same as
g any other card—seat it in an empty slot and screw it to the case. But sound cards are noto-
side effects: interference with modems, NIC cards, and other peripherals. In this lab, you'll
w to install an audio card, connect it to a CD or DVD drive, and install the sound card's

drivers and utilities. But if your sound card fails to work or interferes with the operation of another peripheral, you'll want to look at Lab 31, which explains how to resolve I/O (input/output) address conflicts.

Exercise

To Install a Sound Card

1. Turn off the computer, unplug all external cables, and open the case.

2. Make notes describing the positions of any switches, jumper plugs, or other settings on the sound card.

NOTE Some sound cards are very particular, and very demanding, about their relationship to the operating system. One sound card uses *two* DMA channels and *three* I/O addresses! This is why you want to make good notes about your sound card's requirements.

---

3. Find out what kind of slot your sound card uses. It probably requires a PCI slot, but check the documentation—or look at the card itself—to make sure.

WARNING Never plug a card into the wrong kind of slot. It's possible, physically, to stick a PC card into an ISA slot. But when you turn on the power, you're likely to ruin the card and possib damage your motherboard! PCI slots are shorter than ISA slots, and PCI slots are lighter color than ISA slots. Most of today's computers have both kinds of slots, so you'll want to know how identify them.

---

4. Gently push the sound card into a slot.

5. Following the instructions in the sound card's manual, attach the card to powered speaker to a receiver by plugging a stereo audio cord into the back of the sound card.

6. Plug in the audio cable between your sound card and the CD or DVD drive. Check the card's instructions for the location of its CD audio receptacle. If you find two CD audio tacles, use the one named "In 1" or some other label involving the number 1.

7. Power up the computer. After Windows starts, it will likely inform you that it is auto-d new hardware (Windows 98/NT/2000 featuring Plug and Play).

8. Follow the instructions Windows provides to install the sound card's driver and any additional utility or application software that comes with your card.

9. Reboot the computer when instructed during the Setup process; then when Windows restarts, you should hear the chord that announces Windows. If you don't hear this sound, see the next section.

To Fix Sound Card Problems

1. If your sound card isn't working, first check to make sure that there are no physical problems with the card. See whether power is turned on to the powered speakers (or receiver) attached to your sound card. And if you are using a receiver, check to see that its input selection switch is set to the input where you plugged in the cord coming from the back of the sound card. You may have used the CD-In or Aux-In plug on the receiver. If you did, ensure that the receiver's input select switch points to CD-In or Aux-In.

2. Ensure that the audio cord between the sound card and your powered speakers or receiver is properly inserted at both ends.

3. Double-click the Sounds icon in Control Panel. The Sounds Properties dialog box opens.

4. At this point you're going to trigger a sound to see if the preceding steps solved your problem. In the Schemes drop-down list box, select a scheme.

5. Click the button with a right-pointing arrow next to the Preview icon. If you hear a sound, your card is working correctly.

6. If you are still experiencing problems with your sound card, see Lab 31 or Lab 35.

DTE Quite a few sound cards are set at the factory to IRQ 7, which is unfortunate because that ꭍ is also the default for most printers (IRQ 7 is assigned to the first parallel port, LPT1). However, ꭍ usually won't notice this IRQ conflict because Windows 95/98/2000 or Windows NT all see the ꭍflict when a sound card is installed and attempt (and usually succeed) to reassign the sound ꭍ to a different IRQ. For more on IRQ conflicts, see Lab 35.

Most sound cards default to I/O address 220, and (as with IRQs) only one device at a time ꭍassigned to a particular I/O address. Windows attempts to resolve these address conflicts, ꭍt if the problem persists, see Lab 31.

Lab 30

DATE _____ NAME _____

1. Does it matter if you plug a PCI card into an ISA slot? If so, why?

_____

_____

_____

_____

2. Describe the purpose of CD audio receptacles. If your sound card has two CD audio receptacles, which one should you use?

_____

_____

_____

_____

_____

3. If you hear no sounds coming from your receiver, why should you check the receiver's input select switch?

_____

_____

_____

_____

_____

4. If you're having problems getting your sound card to work, what steps should you take using the Windows Control Panel?

_____

_____

_____

_____

Lab 31: Handling I/O Address Conflicts

Objectives for This Lab

Upon completion of this lab, you will be able to

1. Resolve an address conflict that interferes with your boot drive, causing your computer to fail to boot.

2. Resolve an address conflict among three peripherals competing for the same I/O address range.

Hardware & Software Requirements

Hardware:

1. A working PC computer

2. An installed Ethernet card using address 330

3. A SCSI host adapter using address 330

4. A Sound Blaster 16 sound card (or some other card that defaults to I/O address 330)

Software:

1. The drivers and utilities that come with the Sound Blaster 16 (or other card)

2. The manuals for the Ethernet card using the SCSI host adapter and the Sound Blaster 16 (or other) sound card

What to Read in the Book

Chapter 5, pages 338–41, *The Complete PC Upgrade & Maintenance Guide*, Mark Minasi, Sybex

Introduction

With the arrival of Plug and Play, the problems associated with getting peripherals to work together harmoniously inside a computer were supposed to vanish.

And they're supposed to. Unfortunately, design flaws in the original PC specifications have been compounded over time by the unwillingness of some peripheral manufacturers to play by the rules of good computer citizenship. Some manufacturers have unique ways of routing their data; others insist on hogging resources needed by other hardware; yet others insist on using *a particular I/O address and only that I/O address*. You can imagine what happens if two peripherals insist on the same I/O address. You may have seen this phenomenon when two people insist on occupying the same window seat on an airplane—a fight can break out.

For example, the computer has two easily usable COM ports: COM1 and COM2. COM1 is generally used by the mouse, and COM2 is generally reserved for the modem. COM1 uses up I/O addresses 3F9–3FF. What if another peripheral is hard-wired to require addresses 3F9–3FF? (In some cases you can change the DMA and IO address for the device, and you can leave the mouse where it is. See Lab 31.) You typically have to either move the mouse to a different connector or return that other demanding peripheral to the store. Fortunately, most sound cards default to address 220, and most also permit you to redefine their address if 220 is already in use by some other hardware in the system. Also, fortunately, certain addresses are well known—the addresses for COM1, COM2, and the keyboard are *never* used by peripheral manufacturers other than those making mice, modems, and keyboards, respectively.

I/O addresses are similar to Post Office boxes. You've seen them: numbered boxes covering entire walls, each box given a different number (its address). Let's imagine that the keyboard sends your keystrokes into Box 64. As soon as the computer's CPU gets some free time, it checks Box 64 to see whether any keystrokes have been stored there. To the CPU, the keyboard itself is an abstraction. The CPU thinks of Box 64 as the virtual keyboard because that's where any keyboard data always resides.

Now you run down to your computer store, your tail wagging, to buy the latest, greatest DVD drive! You can't wait to play DVD movies on your monitor or a nearby TV, and play the latest mega-memory games as well. You carefully remove the old CD drive and, following all the right steps (Lab 25), you install the new DVD drive. You turn on the power. The DVD drive doesn't work, and now even your *keyboard* isn't working either! The problem? It's likely that the DVD drive is set to use address 64. Given that (in this example) your keyboard also uses I/O address 64, both devices fail. *Two peripherals cannot run using the same I/O address.* (In some cases you may have to change the I/O address by adjusting jumpers on the card itself.)

No sane hardware manufacturers are going to let their peripherals use address 64. Everyone knows that 64 is already in use by the keyboard. Because every PC has a keyboard, and because every keyboard uses address 64, this address has become well-known forbidden territory. But what about scanners, video capture boards, and other *optional* equipment? For them, the use of I/O addresses is more ambiguous, and conflicts—competitions for the same address—do occur.

In this lab, you'll install a Sound Blaster 16 sound card (or some other card that defaults to I/O address 330) on a computer that contains an Ethernet card and a SCSI host adapter. As you'll see, there be I/O address conflicts that must be resolved.

Exercise

To Resolve an I/O Address Conflict

Some peripheral cards—such as video capture boards—come with self-test programs that check to see if the card is experiencing any memory, interrupt, or I/O address conflicts with other peripherals attached to your computer. Though they're not foolproof, you should certainly run any self-test that is included with a new peripheral you are introducing to your computer. These tests can provide information in solving any conflicts.

1. Install the Sound Blaster 16 sound card (see Lab 30).

2. Reboot your computer, and you'll get a disk boot failure error. There really isn't anything wrong with your boot drive. The problem is that the Sound Blaster 16 sound card's MIDI interface is set by default to I/O address 330. That same address 330 is also in use by the SCSI host adapter. The SCSI host adapter cannot resolve this conflict.

3. You know that your computer is having problems that are likely induced by the sound card you just installed (after all, things were working just fine before you added this new card). Check the documentation of the sound card and also the documentation for the host adapter. You should see that they are both using address 330.

4. Following the instructions in the sound card's manual, change its I/O address. This is done on the hardware. In the case of the Sound Blaster 16, you change a jumper on the card to shift the card's I/O address from 330 down to address 300.

5. After changing the sound card's MIDI interface jumper to resolve the I/O address conflict, turn power on again to reboot the system. The computer boots. Success—or so it would seem.

6. Install the sound card's drivers and utility software, and then attempt to configure the Sound Blaster. The computer booted because you resolved the boot drive's address conflict with the Sound Blaster's default address. But when you try to configure the Sound Blaster, you run into another problem. This time, it's the Ethernet card that's conflicting with your sound card. When you try to test your sound card by making a sound, the message "make a sound" travels to I/O address 300 where the Ethernet card sits. The Ethernet card can make no sense of this request. Also, when the electric signal is sent out to two devices attempting to share a single address, that signal can become weakened—so weak that it might never even arrive at either the Ethernet card or the sound card.

TIP   As you may recall from Lab 23, standards for SCSI devices and cards are few and far between. There is no standard SCSI host adapter I/O address, so—unlike the well-known keyboard address 64—companies such as Creative Labs (manufacturer of the Sound Blaster) have no way of knowing that your particular SCSI adapter has decided to occupy address 300.

7. Fortunately, your Ethernet card might offer a choice of several addresses: 300, 310, 320, 330, and 340. If so, just set it to 310, for example, and leave the Sound Blaster at 300 and the SCSI host adapter at 330. Now there is peace in the valley at last.

NOTE   Can all address conflicts be resolved? No, but most can. What if your Ethernet card is stubbornly fixed at address 300 in the above example? You cannot resolve that problem. You might have to simply return one of the conflicting boards to the store and shop for a board with address settings that are more flexible.

Lab 31

DATE _____ NAME _____

1. Can a sound card comfortably share the I/O address space for COM1? Why or why not?

_____

_____

_____

_____

_____

2. If you get a boot failure problem when you try to reboot after installing a new peripheral card, what should you suspect is the problem? What is the solution?

_____

_____

_____

_____

_____

_____

_____

3. Describe two problems that can occur if an Ethernet card and an audio card are both sharing address 300, and the audio card starts playing music.

_____

_____

_____

_____

_____

4. How standardized are the addresses used by SCSI devices?

_____

_____

_____

_____

Lab 32: The Device Manager

Objectives for This Lab

Upon completion of this lab, you will be able to

1. Examine the status of the various devices with the Device Manager.

2. Change the settings and update the drivers of the various devices.

Hardware & Software Requirements

Hardware: A PC computer with Windows

Software: None for this lab

What to Read in the Book

Chapter 33, pages 1389–91, *The Complete PC Upgrade & Maintenance Guide,* Mark Minasi, Sybex

Introduction

The Device Manager is a Windows 95/98 utility that displays all the devices Windows has detected and configured, and that allows you to edit the properties of these devices. Device Manager also helps you add or update the drivers of these devices, adjust system resources, make IRQ and I/O settings, and so on. It contains all the active hardware Windows has found and configured.

To start the Device Manager, open the Control Panel (Start ➤ Settings ➤ Control Panel) and double-click the System icon. Alternatively, you can right-click the My Computer icon and select Properties from the shortcut menu. When the System Properties dialog box appears, click the Device Manager tab. If you're using Windows 2000, select the Hardware tab on the System Properties dialog box and click the Device Manager button.

As shown in Figure 32.1, the Device Manager window displays all the devices on the computer. The two option buttons allow you to view devices by Type (listed by their hardware category), or by Connection (listed by the port or device they're connected to).

FIGURE 32.1 Viewing devices in the Device Manager by type

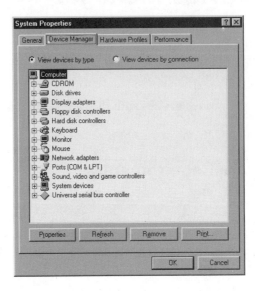

The Remove button allows you to remove a device from the system. If you select a device and then click the Remove button, the Device Manager will uninstall the software needed to support the device, and you can remove the corresponding physical device the next time you turn off the computer.

The Refresh button refreshes the list based on the status of the devices on the system at the moment.

To view the properties of a device, select it with the mouse and click the Properties button, or double-click the name of the device. The hard drives currently installed, for example, are listed under Disk Drives. To see their names and model numbers, click the plus sign in front of the Disk Drives item. Then, to view the properties of a hard drive, double-click its name.

If you're using the Device Manager that comes with Windows 2000, you won't see any buttons, just the names of the devices. Select the name of the device you want to uninstall (or whose properties you want to view) and then click the appropriate button on the toolbar (or right-click the device name and select the desired command from the shortcut menu).

The Properties window for a device contains three (or sometimes four) tabs:

General On this tab you can enable or disable the device and get some information about the manufacturer, the hardware version, and the device status.

Driver On this tab is information about the driver files used by the selected device, including the file's name, location, and version. Use the Update Driver button at the bottom of the dialog box to install

210

a newer version of the driver. The Device Manager can look for a more recent driver on one of the local drives or on the Microsoft Web site (provided you're connected to the Internet, of course).

Resources   On this tab you can see the system resources used by the selected device. If the device conflicts with another, you can change the resource settings on this tab.

Settings   This tab appears with a few devices only. For communications ports, this tab is called Port Settings.

Troubleshooting

If there's a problem with a specific device, its icon in the Device Manager's window will be marked with either an exclamation mark, a question mark, or a red X icon:

- The exclamation mark indicates a problem with the specific device. A description of the problem appears in the General tab of the device's Properties.

- The question mark (also known as splat) indicates that the device is not properly configured.

- The red X indicates a disabled device, one that is physically present in the system and consuming resources but that does not have a driver loaded.

When a specific device is working properly, the message

```
The device is working properly
```

will be printed in the General tab of the device's Properties window. If not, you'll see an error message. Here are a few of the error descriptions that may appear:

```
This device is not configured correctly.
```

> **Solution:** Try to update the drivers for this device by clicking the Update Driver button. If that doesn't work, see your hardware documentation for more information. You can remove the device and let Windows install it, if it's a Plug-and-Play device. Windows will look for the proper driver on the Windows CD. If it's not a PnP device, use the CD or floppies that came with the device.

```
The driver for this device may be bad, or your system may be running low
on memory or other resources.
```

> **Solution:** Update the drivers to see if that fixes the problem. To check your computer's memory and system resources, right-click My Computer on your desktop, click Properties, and then open the Performance tab. If the new driver didn't help, click the Remove button to remove the device and then run the Add New Hardware tool in Control Panel. For older devices, always visit the manufacturer's Web site to see if a newer driver exists for the operating system you're using.

The driver for this device requested a resource that Windows does not know how to handle.

> **Solution:** To fix this, click Update Driver to update the driver for the device. Alternatively, you can click the Remove button and then use the Add New Hardware tool in Control Panel to reinstall the device.

Another device is using the resources this device needs.

> **Solution:** There's a conflict between this device and another one. The quick fix is to remove the other device and restart the computer. The current device will then be able to use the resources it needs. Hopefully, the other device will select different resources when it's installed again. If not, you must manually change the resources. This means you may have to open the computer and set some jumpers on the motherboard or an expansion board. See the documentation of the current device for more information.

This device is not working properly because the BIOS in the device is reporting the resources for the device incorrectly.

> **Solution:** This message tells you that the Registry contains invalid information for this device. It may be possible to resolve the error by removing the device and then installing it again with the Add New Hardware wizard. If not, there's a chance that the device doesn't work under the operating system, or the device or its driver is malfunctioning. Visit the manufacturer's Web site for information on installing and troubleshooting.

This device is either not present, not working properly, or does not have all the drivers installed.

> **Solution:** Make sure the device is connected, and update the driver. If this doesn't help, remove the device and install it again.

The drivers for this device need to be reinstalled.

or

The drivers for this device are not installed.

> **Solution:** Click the Reinstall Driver button in the device's Properties dialog box to again install the drivers for this device.

This device is disabled because the BIOS for the device did not give it any resources.

> **Solution:** You must enable the device in the BIOS. See your hardware documentation for details. Sometimes a USB device may not be working because USB is not enabled in the BIOS.

> This device is using an Interrupt Request (IRQ) resource that is in use
> by another device and cannot be shared. You must change the conflicting
> setting or remove the real-mode driver causing the conflict.

Solution: This means an IRQ cannot be shared; it can originate in the SCSI controller, or the infrared port that uses the same IRS as the serial port. To resolve this error code, remove the real-mode driver that is using the same IRQ as this device. The real-mode driver may be loading in the `CONFIG.SYS` or `AUTOEXEC.BAT` file.

Exercise

To View and Set the CD-ROM's Properties

1. Select the CD-ROM device in the Device Manager and click the Properties button. In the Properties window select the Settings tab.

2. Notice the box Current Drive Letter Assignment. Here you can set the CD-ROM drive's letter. The reason for doing so is that Windows may not recognize some devices if the CD-ROM drive has taken the first available letter after the hard drives. For example, if you install an external Zip drive, you may have to change the letter of the CD-ROM drive in the Device Manager.

To Remove Unused Devices and Drivers

1. Select the Mouse item in the Device Manager's window and expand it.

2. On many computers you'll see the names of several mouse devices, because most users don't remove the driver of an earlier mouse when they install a new one.

3. Select all the mouse devices with an exclamation mark in front of their name, and remove them by clicking the Remove button. You may actually see the same device name (the WheelMouse, for example) repeated, each time with a different port (COM1 or PS/2). Delete all the entries except for the one that corresponds to your mouse and correct port. If you remove the current device's drivers by mistake, you can always reinstall the device.

To View Drives and Partitions

1. Expand the node Disk Drives and you'll see all the drives installed on your system. Select the hard drive (or one of the hard drives) and click Properties.

2. When the Properties window of the selected drive appears, examine the contents of the Current Drive Letter Assignment field. If the entire drive is partitioned as a single drive, you'll see one drive letter. If the physical drive you selected is partitioned in multiple logical drives, you'll see a list of all logical drives, separated with commas.

Lab 32

DATE _____ NAME _____

1. Describe the basic operations you can initiate from within the Device Manager.

_____

_____

_____

_____

_____

2. Describe how you can change the settings of the serial port from within the Device Manager.

_____

_____

_____

_____

_____

3. What's the most common remedy for a device that doesn't work properly?

_____

_____

_____

_____

Lab 33: Using the Add New Hardware Wizard

Objectives for This Lab

Upon completion of this lab, you will be able to install older devices that do not work with Plug and Play, or that Plug and Play fails to handle correctly.

Hardware & Software Requirements

Hardware:

1. A working PC computer

2. A new hardware device that you want to add to the computer

Software: The drivers that come on a CD or diskette with the new hardware device that you are adding to your computer

What to Read in the Book

Chapter 33, pages 1368–74, *The Complete PC Upgrade & Maintenance Guide,* Mark Minasi, Sybex

Introduction

In various labs of this book, we've wistfully mentioned PnP (Plug and Play). Truly, everyone hopes that eventually hardware devices will be able to identify themselves when they are plugged in. The operating system will detect them as soon as they are plugged in. The OS will say, "Hey, you're new. What I/O address do you want, which IRQ? Any other special needs? How about memory requirements?" Then the OS will make arrangements to fit the newcomer into the system—perhaps even installing its drivers from a database of drivers already stored on the hard drive (as is now possible with printers) or on the Internet. Maybe the OS will even reassign an existing device's IRQ or I/O address to make room for the new device. Maybe.

We've used the words *wistfully* and *eventually* in the preceding paragraph because the PnP reality isn't yet equal to the dream. You still sometimes have to adjust rocker switches, DIP switches, jumpers, or other on-card devices that change the I/O address or other resources required by the card. Sometimes there is even a problem with a PnP driver.

And you still sometimes have to try to work out hardware conflicts by using the Add New Hardware Wizard in the Windows Control Panel. This latter task is the subject of this lab. Some boards, or boardless peripherals such as mice, might still need a little help. They may *say* Plug and Play on their box, but you can still have troubles.

If you plug a new peripheral's board into your computer, but Windows doesn't notice it—and it just doesn't *play*—try the Add New Hardware utility. It will probably solve your problems.

Exercise

To Install New Hardware When Plug and Play Fails to Work

NOTE   The steps taken by Windows's Add New Hardware Wizard are quite similar in Windows 95, 98, NT, and 2000. However, they differ in a couple of particulars. If you're using Windows 95, you'll click Next a little less often than when using the later versions of Windows (as described in this lab). The steps are essentially the same, but the Wizard in Windows 95 has fewer pages.

1. Install a peripheral board that is not recognized by Plug and Play into your computer. This can be a legacy board so old that it doesn't feature PnP, or a new, PnP-capable board that, for various reasons, fails to automatically install.

2. After installing the card, reboot your computer. (You might have to wait a minute or two—the detection process is not usually instantaneous.) In this exercise, we assume that Windows doesn't notice the new peripheral at all, or reports that it *does* detect something new but cannot automatically configure it.

3. Double-click the Add New Hardware icon in Control Panel. The Add New Hardware Wizard fires up and requests that you close any currently running applications.

4. Close any currently running applications other than the Add New Hardware Wizard. (Setup utilities always ask you to do this, by the way, because it might be necessary to upgrade a driver in use by a currently running application. And if a driver is in use, it cannot be replaced.)

5. Click the Next button twice. At this point, the Wizard checks for any new PnP devices that have been added to your computer. This process freezes the machine temporarily and can also (sometimes) blank the screen. Sit patiently until the Wizard returns to your screen and the computer unfreezes.

6. You are now given the option of either having Windows automatically search for non-PnP devices, or choosing your device from a list. Choose the automatic search and click Next. You are warned that the computer may freeze, and that the process of searching can take a while.

7. Click Next, and the automatic search for non-PnP hardware begins. Windows is generally fairly good at detecting legacy devices, so let it do its search. If it does recognize the device, Windows will either automatically install the necessary driver(s) from its own database, or will request that you insert the diskette or CD that came with the new device. If you don't have the diskette or CD, you can try getting the driver(s) online from the manufacturer's Web site. See the sidebar about downloading driver updates.

8. If the new device still can't be located, click Next; you'll be given the opportunity to locate your new device in a list (the same option you did *not* choose in step 6 above).

TIP The Wizard is fallible; it's a wizard, not a genius. Sometimes it finds the wrong thing and other times it fails to find anything at all. For instance, if you've installed new hardware that wants to use IRQ 15 and you already have hardware using that interrupt, the Wizard will probably fail to install your new peripheral. See the sidebar "Downloading Driver Updates" for a way around this kind of problem.

---

9. Click in the list box to select the kind of device you are installing; then click Next. The Wizard will attempt to help you install the kind of device you have selected. Windows builds a driver database and then displays a list of drivers it has for the type of device you have selected. If your model or brand is not listed in the Windows driver database, click the Have Disk button to add the necessary driver(s) from the CD or diskette supplied by the manufacturer of your device.

10. After the driver(s) and other support software are installed, you might be asked to specify which COM port or printer port you want to attach the device to. You may also be asked to configure the port or specify other information about your device. Follow the Wizard's suggestions and refer to your new hardware's manual as you complete the installation and testing process.

TIP **Got a Conflict?** Here's another trick you can try if you suspect a conflict when installing a new device. Sometimes the Add New Hardware wizard cannot precisely detect a newly installed peripheral because there is a device conflict. If you can figure out which existing device is conflicting with the new one you're trying to install, try removing the existing device from the system and then reboot your machine. Now double-click the System icon in Control Panel and go to the Device Manager tab. Find the device you removed, right-click it, and select Remove from the pop-up menu. Restart the PC with the new device installed. At this point, it's likely that Windows will be able to detect and install your new device. Once the new device is working, you can reinstall the conflicting device. It's likely that Windows will assign the old device to different resources than what it was using before, thereby resolving the conflict.

Downloading Driver Updates

You can often improve the behavior of a peripheral by upgrading its driver. Manufacturers sometimes work and rework their drivers to get the best possible performance and most stable functioning out of their product. Also, when you upgrade to a new operating system—from Windows 98, say, to 2000—you might want to get the latest drivers for your hardware. And when you add a new peripheral, you might want to get its latest driver even if Windows has a driver for it in the Windows database, or even if the peripheral came with a CD or diskette containing a driver (there's no telling how long the hardware sat in the store). So go online and locate the manufacturer's Web site. Most manufacturers offer their latest drivers (and other support software) free for downloading.

One final word to the wise: Be sure to use your antivirus program to check any newly downloaded driver, just to be on the safe side.

Lab 33

DATE _____ NAME _____

1. In theory, what jobs should Plug and Play be able to accomplish when you're adding a new
   hardware device?

   _____

   _____

   _____

   _____

   _____

   _____

2. When using the Add New Hardware Wizard, why should you shut down all currently running
   programs?

   _____

   _____

   _____

   _____

   _____

3. Describe three places where a driver for a new hardware device can be located. What is the best source for the latest version of a driver?

_____

_____

_____

_____

_____

4. What is likely to happen if an existing device is using the same IRQ that the new device you're installing wants to use?

_____

_____

_____

_____

Lab 34: Troubleshooting Printers

Objectives for This Lab

Upon completion of this lab, you will be able to

1. Use various tests, techniques, and substitutions to find out why a printer is misbehaving.

2. Fix the printer.

Hardware & Software Requirements

Hardware:

1. A working PC computer

2. An installed printer

Software: The CD or diskette that came with the printer

What to Read in the Book

Chapters 18 and 19, *The Complete PC Upgrade & Maintenance Guide*, Mark Minasi, Sybex

Introduction

For the most part, today's printers are pretty reliable. Of course, as with any other electromechanical device, things can go awry from time to time. And when they do, the steps described in this lab are likely to solve your problem. These steps are necessarily generic—there are hundreds of printing devices in use today. But we think you'll find most of these procedures useful as you narrow down a printer problem and then fix it.

Exercise

To Fix a Printer Problem

1. Make sure that the printer is plugged in and turned on.

2. Make sure that it has paper.

3. Most printers have a self-test feature. Check the printer's manual and try to run that self-test. Many printers are able to describe their own problems—either by reporting an error message back to Windows, displaying a message in the printer's LCD window, or flashing combinations of panel lights. If your printer has a configuration menu, you might want to make a paper copy of it. It should include a list of error messages and their meanings (check your printer manual to see if it has this feature).

4. Following the instructions in the printer's manual, check that the software is correctly configured.

5. Consider the cable. First remove both ends of the printer cable and plug them back in again. Try printing now. If that fails, get a new printer cable and swap it out with the older one to see if there's a break in the wires inside the old cable.

6. If the printer is attached to a network, check its IP address and subnet mask on TCP/IP. Also try printing to the same printer, but from a different computer on the same network; this will help you isolate the problem to a particular computer. Finally, check the server queue to see whether a stuck job is holding everything up. If you do find a stuck job, purge the queue.

7. If you've got another printer (the same model), try swapping it with the misbehaving one. If the new printer works, the problem is in the old printer (or possibly the cable plug or power plug wasn't securely attached).

   There is one other possibility you can check. Attach the bad printer to another PC. If the printer then works, check the driver on the original PC.

Lab 34

DATE _____ NAME _____

1. List the ways in which a printer can communicate about a problem it finds following a self-test.

_____

_____

_____

_____

_____

2. What are two problems that can be traced to the printer cable?

_____

_____

_____

_____

_____

3. Name three steps to take when you're having a problem printing to a network printer.

_____

_____

_____

_____

_____

4. If all else fails, try substituting a new printer. What three conclusions are most likely if the new printer works?

_____

_____

_____

_____

Lab 35: Solving IRQ Problems

Objectives for This Lab

Upon completion of this lab, you will be able to

1. Choose an IRQ for a new peripheral you're adding to a computer.

2. Resolve an IRQ conflict between two peripherals competing for the same IRQ.

3. Free up an IRQ by disabling a port or interface that's not actively used.

Hardware & Software Requirements

Hardware:

1. A working PC computer

2. A hardware device with a board that requires an IRQ

3. A Phillips screwdriver

4. An antistatic wrist strap

Software: None for this lab

What to Read in the Book

Chapter 6, pages 351–60, *The Complete PC Upgrade & Maintenance Guide*, Mark Minasi, Sybex

Introduction

Not too long ago, CPUs used to sit around checking all the time to see whether they were needed by peripherals. This checking behavior, called *polling*, was easily designed but wasted a lot of the CPU's time. The CPU was continually checking and rechecking a device to see whether data was coming in from it. You can imagine how many zillions of polls took place between keypresses, even when the typist was a world champ.

Nevertheless, this CPU inefficiency wasn't much of a problem in the old DOS world where most everything happened one event at a time, and the text-based screen display was not really very demanding.

You couldn't be calculating a spreadsheet while simultaneously typing in a word processor. And nobody ever thought of dragging a window around the screen on top of other windows.

With the advent of Windows, though, all this changed. Multitasking and a GUI both demand much of a CPU. The inefficient polling technique became out of the question. Enter IRQ. *IRQ, or interrupt request,* is a hard-wired method of permitting a peripheral to raise its hand and say, "I have need of the CPU."

IRQs are numbered from 0 to 15 (usually 15 is the highest one—the quantity of IRQs can vary). What happens if two or more peripherals send an interrupt request at the same time? The IRQ with the lower number wins, and the higher-numbered IRQ has to wait until the other IRQ is serviced.

Each active IRQ number has an associated utility program. When an IRQ message arrives, an interrupt controller causes the CPU to temporarily stop what it's doing and execute that IRQ's utility program. It might be a utility program that accepts data from the keyboard, or a program that accepts data coming in from the disk controller. After the interrupt, the CPU picks up where it left off before it was interrupted. All this, of course, happens quite fast. And, just as watching more than 20 photo frames per second convinces the eye that it is seeing a motion picture, so, too, do fast interrupts appear to us humans as *multitasking*—several things happening at the same time. In reality, things are happening sequentially down on the CPU level. But it's all so rapid that we experience it as simultaneity.

NOTE Of all resource conflicts, IRQ conflicts are the most common. However, if you don't find an IRQ conflict and there's still a problem, take a look at these other possible sources of conflict: I/O address, DMA channel, ROM addresses, and RAM buffers.

Exercise

To Choose an IRQ for a New Device

TIP Often Windows can automatically assign an IRQ for a new peripheral that you add to your system. You may not need to take the following steps if there are no IRQ conflicts during the automatic installation process (Plug-and-Play detection), or during an installation using Control Panel's Add New Hardware utility. See Chapter 31 for additional information.

---

1. Turn off the computer, unplug any external cables, and open the case. Install a peripheral card that needs an IRQ.

2. Decide which IRQ you can give to this new piece of hardware you're adding to your computer. Check to see what IRQs are already in use by other peripherals in your machine. Some IRQ numbers are typically reserved for standard PC equipment:

IRQ	Reserved For
0	Timer
1	Keyboard
2	Signal interrupts (don't assign any devices to 2; the computer uses IRQ 2 to cascade to IRQs 8–15)
3	COM2
4	COM1
6	Floppy diskette controller
7	LPT1 (printer port)
8	Clock
12	PS/2-type mouse (if your mouse doesn't connect to COM1, it probably uses IRQ 12)
13	Coprocessor
14	Primary hard-drive interface
15	Secondary hard-drive interface

NOTE As you can see, most IRQ numbers are already in use. You can consider using 9, 10, 11, or 5 (this numeric order represents the order of servicing priority these IRQ numbers have). However, if you have a choice, avoid assigning any devices to IRQ 9. It connects to IRQ 2.

3. Set the IRQ you've chosen for your new peripheral (see the manual that comes with the peripheral for the method that must be used to specify the IRQ for the device).

4. Try booting the computer and see whether the new device is working correctly. If it isn't, the IRQ you chose may already be in use by another device. In Control Panel, double-click the System icon; in the System Properties dialog box, click the Device Manager tab. Right-click the Computer icon in the list box, and click the Properties button. Click the View Resources tab and then the IRQ option button. You'll now see a list box displaying each IRQ in your system and a description of the device(s) using that IRQ, as shown in Figure 35.1.

F I G U R E 35.1   This list describes how each IRQ is currently employed in your computer.

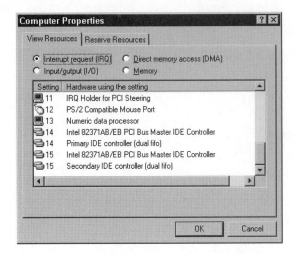

To Resolve an IRQ Conflict

If you've found that you don't have an unused IRQ, here are some steps you can take:

1. Try disabling your parallel port if it's not in use. This will free IRQ 7.

2. If either COM1 or COM2 is not in use, you can free up IRQ 4 or IRQ 3, respectively. You can also disable an unused LPT port through the BIOS.

3. If your system uses PCI (a style of slots that are shorter and lighter-colored than ISA slots), you might be able to set up IRQ sharing through the machine's BIOS. Check your computer's manual.

4. If you have only one hard drive and one CD/DVD drive, you could have them both use the primary EIDE interface (IRQ 14). Then disable the secondary EIDE interface, thereby freeing up IRQ 15 for your use.

WARNING   The solution in step 4 might not be possible on your system. This "sharing the primary interface technique" is easy to accomplish only if the hard drive and CD/DVD drive are on a single interface. Also, some computers will not let you disable the secondary interface.

Lab 35

DATE _____ NAME _____

1. Describe the difference between polling and interrupt requests.

_____

_____

_____

_____

_____

_____

2. What is the significance of IRQ numbers, and how many of them does the average contemporary computer have?

_____

_____

_____

_____

_____

3. Which four IRQ numbers are typically available for your use, and which one of these should you try to avoid?

_____

_____

_____

_____

_____

4. Name two steps you can take to free up IRQ numbers.

_____

_____

_____

_____

_____

Lab 36: Solving Mouse and Keyboard Problems

Objectives for This Lab

Upon completion of this lab, you will be able to

1. Clean a mechanical or optical mouse.

2. Fix a problem keyboard.

Hardware & Software Requirements

Hardware:

1. A working PC computer

2. A keyboard

3. A mouse

4. A photocopier

5. A pencil eraser and tweezers

6. A can of compressed air (available at electronic supply houses or computer stores)

Software: None for this lab

What to Read in the Book

Chapter 22, pages 904–09, 913–14, *The Complete PC Upgrade & Maintenance Guide*, Mark Minasi, Sybex

Introduction

We take them for granted—they come with the computer and we use them every day. They're not very expensive. When they go bad, rich people just buy new ones. If you're less than rich, you'll want to know what to do to fix a bad keyboard or a mouse that doesn't work right. You know a mouse is bad when its screen pointer sometimes doesn't move when you move the mouse. You know the keyboard is bad when a key sticks and won't pop back up, or when pressing a key has no effect. What to do when your mouse or keyboard fails is the subject of this lab. It's a lab about cleanliness.

Exercise

To Clean a Mouse

Mechanical mice have small wheels inside, as well as a strangely heavy hard rubber ball (it has a metal core, like our planet Earth). The wheels get dirt, grease, or hair on them, and the ball can get gummy and slick. This happens to all of us sooner or later. When your mouse gets sick, follow these steps:

1. Open the bottom of the mouse and remove its ball.

2. You can usually clean the ball by rubbing it with a pencil eraser to get rid of any discolored areas. If it's really greasy, try simply washing it with dishwashing detergent, then letting it dry or patting it dry with paper towels.

3. Examine the wheels inside the mouse case. Use tweezers to remove any hair or other foreign matter. Toothpicks, swabs, or other probes can also be used. For really tough jobs, try all-purpose cleaner or alcohol.

NOTE   If you have an optical mouse, simply wipe the sensors clean with a tissue. Also be sure to keep an optical mouse's pad clean so it can sense the grid.

To Fix a Bad Keyboard

1. Unplug the keyboard from the computer.

2. Invert the keyboard onto a copier machine to take a picture of which keys go where, so you can get the keys back into the right locations quickly when you reassemble.

3. Pry off the key tops.

4. Hold the keyboard upside down and use a can of compressed air to blow the keyboard clean. If it's especially dirty, try using a spray cleaner and let it dry.

5. Plug the keytops back in, and then try the keyboard again with the computer.

6. If you're still having problems with only one key, it might be the key's spring. Pull off the keytop. Reattach the spring if necessary. If that's not the problem, try stretching the spring very slightly. The spring's job is to keep the key up until you press it.

7. Still having a problem with your keyboard? It's time to buy a new one.

Lab 36

DATE _____ NAME _____

1. What are the indications that a mouse or keyboard is having problems?

_____

_____

_____

_____

2. What steps should you take to clean the mouse ball?

_____

_____

_____

_____

3. What steps should you take to clean the interior mouse wheels?

_____

_____

_____

_____

4. What should you try if only one key is causing problems?

_____

_____

_____

_____

_____

Lab 37: Power Safety—Line Noise Protection and Battery Backup

Objectives for This Lab

Upon completion of this lab, you will be able to

1. Understand the problems that can be caused by irregularities in the line AC power.

2. Take steps to solve power problems.

3. Know which devices are available to help prevent power line noise and deal with power loss.

Hardware & Software Requirements

Hardware: A working PC computer

Software: None for this lab

What to Read in the Book

Chapter 4, pages 266–71; Chapter 9, pages 472–85, *The Complete PC Upgrade & Maintenance Guide*, Mark Minasi, Sybex

Introduction

Most people think that power arrives, steady and stable, at our houses and businesses. After all, the lights almost always shine evenly and the TV picture doesn't shrink and bloom very often. But the truth is, electricity varies quite a bit. You (and your computer) can suffer from under- or overvoltage problems, brownouts or blackouts, and transients (spikes and surges in power). These variations in power can cause problems for electronic equipment, including computers and their peripherals.

You cannot do much about the power arriving at your building, but you can do plenty once that power gets inside. Conditioners, surge suppressors, and backup batteries are available to help you solve most power supply problems that can affect PCs.

TIP   Power surges are problems for delicate items such as the filament in a lightbulb, or the micro-circuitry in your computer system. There's a very simple way to prevent one common type of power surge: Just leave your computer running all the time. Each time you press the "on" switch to any electric appliance, power gushes into it. Studies show that when you flip the power switch, four to six times the normal current (600 to 900 watts for a PC) briefly flashes into your machine. Many people swear by the theory that electronic equipment should generally be left on all the time to prevent this inrush of current and the havoc it can wreak with delicate intelligent machinery. So turn off the printer and monitor, but leave the computer itself on.

WARNING   Avoid switch flicking. Computers sometimes freeze up, begin redrawing repeated windows, become sluggish, refuse to open a DVD drawer, or otherwise start acting crazy. This sort of problem is usually best fixed by turning off the power, waiting three or four minutes for things to cool down (for the RAM memory chips to completely release their data), and then turning the computer back on. However, some people take this process too far: They turn their computer on and off rapidly several times in a matter of seconds, evidently thinking that this is the computer equivalent of shaking dust out of a mop. What they are actually doing, though, is quite difficult for the computer to bear—it can destroy the power supply.

Signs of a Power Problem

Some computer troubles that might seem unrelated to power actually *are* power related:

- You get odd errors that seem to occur in RAM memory.
- The hard drive loses data mysteriously.
- The computer freezes for no particular reason.
- Circuit board chips are being randomly damaged.
- You get errors or noise when printing, going online, or working with other peripherals.
- The hard drive sometimes boots but sometimes doesn't.
- The keyboard inexplicably stops communicating with the computer now and then.
- The boot sequence memory check strangely stops and freezes.

Exercise

To Solve Power-Related Problems

Perhaps you noticed what most of the problems listed in the "Signs of a Power Problem" sidebar have in common: They are both *strange* and *intermittent*. Here are some steps to take if you suspect power supply problems:

1. Try plugging the computer into a different wall outlet. Sometimes sharing power with Mr. Coffee is all it takes to drive your machine crazy.

2. Have an electrician check to see that your outlets are correctly wired.

3. Ensure that all peripherals share a common ground with the computer.

4. Purchase protection devices to defend your computer and its peripherals against spikes, surges, and over- or undervoltage (see the next section).

Devices to Install to Help Guard Against Power Problems

1. **Surge Protectors:** If you don't consider a particular computer to be mission critical, you can take a chance and purchase one of these inexpensive protection devices.

   You know what these look like—resembling a large, metal- or plastic-boxed extension cord, they have a rocker switch and four or six receptacles. Some have a little light on them that's supposed to go out when they've been zapped, have given up their life, and can no longer protect. The problem with these devices is that they've been professionally tested and found wanting. Some, when trying to block a serious surge (think lightning) go up in flames. Others lose their ability to redirect a surge (to ground), but continue to seem fine—even the little light can continue to shine on top of a dead surge protector. And, once they die, these surge protectors become merely impressive-looking extension cords, offering no defense against surges at all. However, there is one surge protector that can be recommended, built by a company called Zero-Surge (http://www.zerosurge.com/). Though more expensive than common-variety surge protectors, the Zero-Surge devices work well. We really cannot recommend the other surge protectors.

2. **Power Conditioners:** This is the next step up in price (and performance) from inexpensive surge protectors.

   Add a power conditioner to your system if protecting your equipment is highly important to you. A conditioner does everything promised by surge protectors (isolating equipment from line noise dangers), but it also offers superior noise filtering performance. And most models can also keep things in good shape during brownouts by boosting undervoltage. What's more, if a power conditioner fails—can no longer protect your equipment—it lets you know in dramatic fashion: It will no longer pass power, and none of your devices will work.

WARNING   Check the power rating of a power conditioner. You might need to plug your laser printer in elsewhere, because it, alone, can draw up to 15 amps.

3. **A Backup Power Supply:** This is the most expensive solution, but one type of backup supply provides everything offered by a good power conditioner and protects your data from power outages as well. Even a brief interruption in power can wipe out all the data in RAM memory, and you lose whatever work you've done since the last time the data was saved to disk.

Backup power devices come in two flavors:

- A *standby power supply* (SPS) charges its batteries and keeps an eye on the level of the current. If power goes low, the SPS activates itself via a fast switching device and feeds power to the computer system. To do its job correctly with no data loss, you want to ensure that you get an SPS with a switching time of 4 milliseconds or less. Anything slower and you can experience problems.

- An *uninterruptible power supply* (UPS) continually shunts line power into its battery, and then from the battery into the computer system. This arrangement makes a switching device unnecessary, hence the name *uninterruptible*. A UPS acts as a surge suppressor as well, because line surges dump safely into the battery that stands between the wall plug and your computer.

When purchasing a UPS, you can try to get one with sine wave AC current, but it'll be more expensive. If money is a consideration, try getting an SPS with a switching time faster than 4 milliseconds. Note, however, that with an SPS you'll still need to purchase a surge suppressor as well.

TIP   One important consideration: Get a backup power supply that includes a serial port. The operating system can be informed of a power loss via this serial port (with a signal called a "heartbeat"), and can automatically shut down the computer—including safely flushing data from the cache to save it to the disk drive—before the battery power runs out.

WARNING   Some people might try to sell you a device with the oxymoronic name *offline UPS*. Now an offline UPS would be somewhat more useful than a cardboard safe, but they're in the same general category, aren't they?

Lab 37

DATE _____ NAME _____

1. Name four computer problems that might be caused by AC line power faults.

   _____

   _____

   _____

   _____

   _____

   _____

   _____

2. Why is it a good idea for your computer to share a common ground with its peripherals?

   _____

   _____

   _____

   _____

   _____

   _____

   _____

   _____

3. Which kind of backup power supply is the best compromise if money is tight? Which kind is best if the sky's the limit?

_____

_____

_____

_____

_____

4. Describe the differences between a UPS and an SPS.

_____

_____

_____

_____

_____

Lab 38: General Troubleshooting

Objectives for This Lab

Upon completion of this lab, you will be able to

1. Use proven techniques, approaches, and attitudes that will lead to success in solving computer problems.

2. Learn the six basic steps—and the correct order to take those steps—when tackling a computer problem.

Hardware & Software Requirements

Hardware: A PC computer (with a problem that needs to be solved)

Software: Diagnostic software

What to Read in the Book

Chapter 5, *The Complete PC Upgrade & Maintenance Guide*, Mark Minasi, Sybex

Introduction

Over the years, expert PC troubleshooters learn a thing or two. General habits of mind, attitudes, and approaches to computer problem-solving emerge and prove to be of real value. There are also some general steps to take when tackling nearly any kind of PC breakdown. These are the topics of this lab.

Eight Rules for Successful Troubleshooting

Make notes. Always draw diagrams, jot down IRQ settings, sketch the location and position of DIP switches, and record any other information that's not totally obvious whenever you're installing, disassembling, replacing, or otherwise changing things in the PC. *Don't depend on your memory.* After you've got things torn apart, it's usually hard to remember just exactly how they go back together. Some people even use a Polaroid camera to take snapshots of settings and lab configurations. Another useful tactic is to keep a list of all your peripherals' drivers, and store a backup copy of each driver as well.

Work on simpler solutions first.   Don't start fixing a video problem by replacing the motherboard. The motherboard might indeed be the source of the problem, but then again the problem could be the cable, and it's much easier to try reseating the cable or swapping in another known good cable than to swap the motherboard. Moral: List the possible bad hardware and try the easier swaps first.

Try rebooting.   This is an extension of the preceding rule. If something odd happens in the behavior of an application, your first (and easiest) remedy to try is to turn off the power, wait three minutes, and then turn it back on. This fixes any problems in RAM memory caused by power noise or other sources.

Try eliminating complications.   When there's a problem, try to reduce the computer to its bare bones and see if the problem persists. Take the computer off the network (if it's part of a network); disconnect from the Internet; turn off any screen savers and other utility software. In other words, try for as elementary a configuration as possible. Turn off the computer and, during reboot, press F8 to get into Safe mode (a relatively simple version of Windows). Try removing as many services as you can; press Ctrl+Alt+Del in Windows 98, NT, or 2000, and then use the Task Manager to close down nonessential individual services. Tracking down software conflicts is similar to tracking down hardware problems—it's a process of elimination. The fewer programs running while the problem persists, the closer you are to finding the cause of that problem.

Replace the software first.   Make a diagram of the problem. If a printer is failing, draw the items involved in printing: printer, cable, parallel port, motherboard, printer driver(s), application trying to print. In this list of suspects, the easiest to check first is the software. Try reinstalling the printer driver, or using the application's setup or configuration program. Most troubleshooting involves swapping because actually testing individual hardware components requires too much specialized equipment and knowledge. But easier than swapping is fiddling around with software first to see if that's the source of the problem.

Be methodical and scientific.   Just because some software has always been dependable, don't assume it's not the problem. Just because the modem is acting up, don't assume the problem couldn't be interference from the sound card. Never theorize in this fashion: "Why, it could never be the _____" (fill in the blank). If it *possibly* could be the _____, then test it.

Don't completely trust documentation.   You *must* read the manuals and instruction pamphlets that come with your hardware and software to see if the answer to your problem can be found there. But you also *must not* trust that the documents contain no errors. Often the people who know the technical details are not the ones who write the final text. Sometimes a manual tries to cover more than one product in more than one language. Sometimes proofreaders or editors change details best left alone. The opportunities for errors in technical documentation are many.

Don't predict the problem. Never put your reputation behind a particular solution, or you may end up defending your ego instead of locating the true problem. If someone asks you what you think is wrong, reply that you don't have enough information at this point to predict. If you say, "probably the hard drive," you'll unconsciously start looking for *that* solution, to vindicate yourself. This attitude can prolong what might have been a much quicker fix.

Exercise

The General Troubleshooting Process

Following are six steps that you should take to fix most computer problems. And you should take these steps *in this order*:

1. Find out what the *user* is doing. Operator error is usually—in fact nearly always—the problem.

2. Make sure everything is plugged in. In fact, go even further: Power down, then unplug and replug any cords associated in the slightest way with the problem.

3. Check out the software.

4. Look for evidence. Are there strange noises? How are indicator lights on the printer configured (and what does the manual say about these lights)? Look for any out-of-the-ordinary events or signs.

5. Run diagnostic software. There are a number of excellent diagnostic programs that ship with computers, or that you can buy from aftermarket software houses (see pages 306–18 of *The Complete PC Upgrade & Maintenance Guide* for recommended third-party diagnostic software).

NOTE Diagnostic software isn't generally able to describe a problem for you. What it does best is reassure you that various elements of your system are functioning *correctly* and can therefore be eliminated from your list of suspects.

---

6. Check out the hardware. Take the computer apart if necessary. Clean connectors (with an artist's eraser); reseat chips, cards, and internal plugs (both data and power); and generally clean and check the hardware before moving on to the swapping phase, where you actually start substituting devices, plugs, and so on.

Lab 38

DATE _____ NAME _____

1. If the monitor is misbehaving, should you try swapping out the cable first, or the monitor? Why?

_____

_____

_____

_____

_____

_____

2. When attempting to locate the source of a problem, should you check out the hardware before checking out the software?

_____

_____

_____

_____

_____

3. In the troubleshooting process, should you attempt to predict what would probably cure the problem?

_____

_____

_____

_____

_____

4. What aspect of troubleshooting does diagnostic software usually handle best?

_____

_____

_____

_____

Lab 39: Notebook Upgrades

Objectives

Upon completion of this lab, you will be able to

1. Add memory to a notebook computer.

2. Replace the hard disk of a notebook computer.

Hardware & Software Requirements

Hardware: A working notebook computer

Software: The original setup CDs and floppies that came with the notebook; the Windows emergency floppy

What to Read in the Book

Chapter 29, *The Complete PC Upgrade & Maintenance Guide,* Mark Minasi, Sybex

Introduction

As more and more people need to access their data on the go, notebook computers are becoming more and more popular. Many professionals use powerful notebooks that can even double as desktop replacements. As you probably know, notebook computers cannot be repaired or upgraded as easily as desktop computers. If your notebook stops working, your only option is to return it to the manufacturer to be repaired. In terms of upgrading a notebook, there are a few things you can do, and you'll read more about them in the following paragraphs. But there's not much; for example, you can't replace the graphics adapter, and you can't add just any hard drive you may desire.

The problem with notebooks is that they're too compact. Designers try to squeeze as much as possible into the notebook's case. The CPU is soldered on the motherboard, and there's no room to fit expansion cards in the case. Short of adding memory, the only expansion options are the notebook's two PCMCIA slots. As a fortunate result, however, there are practically no conflicts between devices that you have to troubleshoot.

By the same token, upgrades are very simple. You can add memory, replace the existing hard drive or add a second one, and add PCMCIA expansion cards (or PC cards). All expansion and upgrade options are described in detail in the documentation. For anything else, you simply return it to the manufacturer. Because of their limited troubleshooting possibilities, notebooks come with diagnostic software that's customized for the specific model.

CPU Upgrades

Some companies used to offer CPU upgrades for notebooks, but these parts are very hard to find nowadays. Most CPUs in today's notebooks can't be upgraded, for the simple reason that the CPU is soldered onto the motherboard. Besides, the notebook's motherboard was designed for a specific CPU speed, so don't expect that you'll be able to upgrade the CPU of an old notebook. As far as we know, none of the major manufacturers will replace the CPU or the motherboard with a new one.

A very few notebooks have replaceable CPUs (almost none of them are Pentium notebooks). Even these machines must be returned to the manufacturer or a trained vendor for the upgrade.

Batteries

Eventually, you'll have to replace your notebook's battery. You'll know when you need a new battery because the interval between successive charges will become shorter and shorter. You can purchase a battery directly from the manufacturer or from a third company. If you provide the model number (and perhaps the information printed on the battery), you'll get the right battery. Some battery models are discontinued very soon after their release, and you may find it hard to find a replacement, so it's a good idea to purchase a second battery and keep it on hand. It will prove invaluable on long trips, and it may give continued life to your notebook if the original battery dies.

NOTE When you purchase a new notebook computer, the battery is completely discharged. You should *not* use the computer immediately (as many people do). Leave the computer plugged in but turned off for a few hours, until the battery is completely charged. Consult the documentation to find out how long it takes to charge the battery for the first time. Most notebooks are equipped with special indicators that let you know when the battery is charging and when it's full.

Exercise

To Replace the Battery

The first item that will eventually fail in your notebook is the battery, and it's no surprise that the battery is the simplest part to replace. To replace it (or to remove it, if you plan to leave the computer idle for more than a few weeks), follow these steps:

1. Turn off the notebook computer and disconnect the AC adapter.

2. Locate the battery compartment. The compartment's latch is usually on the bottom of the computer. In some notebooks the battery is hidden under the keyboard, and you'll have to lift the keyboard in order to reach the battery. You'll find detailed diagrams for removing the battery in the notebook's documentation.

3. Once you open the battery compartment, the only item you'll see there is the battery. It will either slide out or have a tab you can lift to remove the battery.

4. Take out the old battery, insert the new one, and close the compartment. Then plug in the AC adapter and turn on the computer.

NOTE Don't throw the old battery in the garbage can. Use the special battery disposal can at your favorite electronics store.

To Add and Remove PCMCIA Cards

The most popular PCMCIA cards are modems and LAN adapters. Modems are indispensable for any computer, including notebooks. LAN cards allow you to synchronize a notebook with a desktop computer. You can even find a hard drive in the form of a PCMCIA card and increase your notebook's capacity considerably. Unfortunately, these cards are Type III cards and each one takes up both PCMCIA slots in the notebook. Moreover, their capacity is quite small compared to the near-20GB hard drives you get with a high-end notebook.

PCMCIA cards can be inserted and removed while the notebook is on. You'll need to first stop the card before removing it; to do so, use the PC Card Status utility.

1. Locate the PC Card Status icon in the system tray on the desktop. It's usually a small icon of a PCMCIA card.

2. Double-click the icon to display the PC Card (PCMCIA) Properties dialog box, shown in Figure 39.1.

3. Look for an icon for each PCMCIA card in the computer. Select the one you want to stop and click the Stop button.

4. Several seconds later, the card's description on the dialog box will change to "Empty," and a message box will notify you that it's safe to remove the card.

249

5. To activate the card again, you must pull it out and reinsert it. Notice that there's no Start button, and the notebook will not recognize the card unless it's extracted and inserted again.

F I G U R E   39.1   Use the PCMCIA Card Properties dialog box to stop a PCMCIA card before removing it.

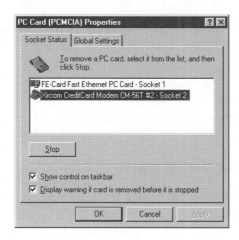

NOTE   PCMCIA cards are Plug-and-Play devices, and Windows will recognize them as soon as you insert them. It will attempt to install the required drivers automatically, but you may need to insert the card's CD or diskette.

To Add Memory to Your Notebook

Adding memory is the most frequent upgrade people perform on a notebook computer. Each manufacturer uses its own design, and you must consult the documentation to find out how to reach the memory slots. Nearly all notebooks have two memory slots, at least one of them already populated. If both slots are populated, you'll have to remove one of the modules.

Notebook memory modules are neither SIMMs nor DIMMs. They are proprietary modules and they probably won't fit in another maker's machine. Figure 39.2 shows two typical 16MB memory modules. One of them is seated firmly in its slot, and the other has been inserted but needs to be pushed down to latch in the slot.

FIGURE 39.2   Typical notebook memory modules

1. First, buy the module you need. Since notebook memory modules are proprietary, you may not find a module with the exact capacity you want. When deciding how much memory you'll need, keep in mind that after the installation, there will be no more memory slots available for future expansion. Be sure to select a module you won't have to replace in a few months.

NOTE   The best place to purchase memory modules for your notebook is from the vendor that sold you the notebook. You can also buy memory modules from other suppliers. Because memory modules are made for specific makes and models, you only need to specify the notebook's model when you order. It wouldn't hurt to verify that the module's speed is within the range specified by the notebook's manufacturer. Notebook memory modules are more expensive than the DIMM chips you use with your desktop, so be prepared to spend a little more.

2. The compartment containing the memory modules is usually located at the bottom or side of the notebook's case. Sometimes the memory modules are placed under the keyboard. If you have to lift the keyboard to reach the memory modules, do so very carefully because the cable that connects it to the motherboard is very short. Locate the memory compartment using the notebook's documentation, and then open it.

3. If you have to remove a memory module and replace it with a higher-capacity one, follow the manufacturer's instructions. In general, you'll need to locate two very small tabs on either side

of the module and press them outward or downward to release the module. Once the module clicks, you can pull it out of the slot.

4. Insert the new module. Again, consult the documentation for the exact procedure. In most cases, you'll have to insert the module at an angle and then press it to latch.

5. Carefully close the computer and turn it on. If the computer doesn't see the additional memory, open the notebook again and make sure the module sits firmly in its slot. If everything seems OK, try switching the two memory modules. If the computer still doesn't see any memory after the swapping of the modules, chances are that the new module is malfunctioning.

To Replace the Hard Disk

Costlier notebooks accept a second hard drive, which fits in the same slot as the floppy drive, the CD-ROM, or even the power supply. Practically speaking, this means you'll need to remove one of the other storage devices in order to add a second drive. The floppy drive is the first peripheral you can live without. Most people use the Internet and LANs to exchange files with others. When you do need to store data on a disk, chances are you'll use a backup device such as the Iomega Zip drive.

Most notebooks, however, do not support two hard drives, and you'll have to remove the existing hard drive and replace it with another, high-capacity one. Here are the steps for doing that:

1. First, purchase the new drive. As is true for buying memory, the notebook's manufacturer is the best choice when you buy a new drive. You can also purchase it from a third-party supplier for a little less. To specify the type of drive, you'll only need to identify the notebook's model number.

2. Locate the compartment of the hard drive. On many notebooks you can access the drive through a small door on the side of the computer and slide it out. Each manufacturer uses a different mechanism to hold the drive in place, so consult the notebook's manual for specific instructions.

   Figure 39.3 shows a slim-line hard drive. Notice the single connector on the hard drive. There are no cables to be plugged; you simply slide the drive into the bay. Most drives are powered by three contacts on the drive itself—this explains why there's no power connector.

F I G U R E   39.3   A typical slim-line hard drive

3. Before inserting the new drive, read the documentation to understand the mechanism that holds the drive in place. Many drives have a metal lever that must be pushed down after you insert the drive into the bay. Other drives use a small latch, while still others must be screwed into place.

4. The next step is to configure the drive. Fortunately, you don't have to do much. The notebook drives come preconfigured, and you won't have to set any DIP switches on the drive or the motherboard.

   Many notebooks include a utility that will automatically partition and format the new drive. If the new drive replaces an existing one, you must install the operating system from scratch. Again, many notebooks come with a CD that copies all the necessary files on the hard disk.

Lab 39

DATE _____ NAME _____

1. Write down the maximum amount of memory you can add to your notebook computer, as well as the number of slots it has.

   _____

   _____

   _____

   _____

   _____

2. How many storage devices can you fit in your notebook? (Do not count any devices that connect to the parallel port.)

   _____

   _____

   _____

   _____

Lab 40: Building the Ultimate Computer

Objectives for This Lab

Upon completion of this lab, you will be able to

1. Select the parts you need.

2. Put them together to build your dream computer.

Hardware & Software Requirements

Hardware:

1. A computer case with power supply

2. A new motherboard

3. A video card

4. One or more new or used hard drives

5. A modem

6. An antistatic wrist strap, needle-nose pliers, screwdrivers, and a retrieving tool

Software: A Windows original installation CD

What to Read in the Book

Chapter 32, *The Complete PC Upgrade & Maintenance Guide,* Mark Minasi, Sybex

Introduction

Many users build their own custom computers because they want to be able to select the best parts (and replace them with even better parts when those become available). Understandably, the first and most important step in building the ultimate computer is selecting the ultimate parts. Research the market a little, read some trade magazines, and visit your local computer store before you make up your mind. Any book that tells you about the ultimate parts is becoming out of date the moment it's written, let alone when it reaches the local bookstore. In the following sections, we'll give you a few tips, but we won't tell you what's the "ultimate" (if there is such a thing).

The Case

Most people use tower cases (the ones that stand on the floor next to your desk). The case should be roomy so that it can accommodate all the devices you want to put in it today and, perhaps, a year or two from now. It's likely that you'll revise your design of the ultimate computer and replace parts (or add new ones) every six months. The one thing you need not replace is the motherboard—at least, not before all components are miniaturized beyond recognition. So buy a computer case that can accommodate many drives and expansion cards.

There are two things to look for in a computer case: the location of the power supply and the frame that holds the drives. The power supply should be located near the top of the case. The fan pulls hot air out of the unit, and you don't want the hot air to circulate around the CPU or the memory. In some tower cases the power supply is at the bottom, next to the motherboard, and this isn't a bad or unusual design. The frame that holds the drives should be accessible from both sides so that you can remove all the screws that hold the drives to the frame. We've seen frames in which you must remove the motherboard before you can even see the screws. Avoid them.

The Motherboard and CPU

A very important part is the motherboard. Buy anything less than state-of-the-art and you'll have to replace it real soon. Along with the motherboard comes the BIOS, so be sure to buy a motherboard with a brand-name BIOS such as Award or Phoenix. Also make sure that the BIOS can be easily upgraded (some type of flash memory is ideal). Finally, visit the BIOS manufacturer's Web site to find out the latest version of the BIOS. If this version isn't available with the motherboard you want to buy, ask how you can upgrade it. Don't hesitate to ask hard questions. You may find that a specific motherboard doesn't support the latest features of the BIOS.

All motherboards have built-in controllers for the floppy drives, hard drives, and serial and parallel ports, and the most modern ones also have USB ports. Many motherboards also include a built-in video controller, but in most cases it's not state-of-the-art. If you're happy with the on-board video controller, use it. If you later decide to upgrade the video controller, you can purchase a video expansion card and disable the on-board video circuitry (either by setting a jumper or through the BIOS Setup program). The USB port is also important. Don't buy a motherboard without a USB port (two is better).

The most important motherboard specification is the speed of the bus. Older motherboards run at 66MHz; nowadays you can get them at 100MHz and even 133MHz. The faster the motherboard, the better. Of course, you'll have to purchase costlier memory modules to make the most of the bus speed, but you wouldn't skimp on the memory, would you?

The speed of the motherboard is (practically) independent of the processor's speed. You can have a 100MHz motherboard with a 500MHz Pentium. You'll simply set the multiplier to 5 ($5 \times 100 = 500$MHz). Each motherboard, however, can accommodate CPUs up to a maximum speed, so make sure this speed is as high as it can be. If you plan to purchase a 450MHz CPU, the motherboard should be able to accommodate at least a 600MHz CPU because that is the speed of the CPU you'll be using next year. (The topic of bus speed and the multiplier was discussed in Lab 9.) On most motherboards, the speed of the CPU (which is determined by the speed of the bus and the multiplier) is set through special jumpers. The newest motherboards allow you to set the speed of the bus and the multiplier through the BIOS.

100 or 133 MHz is plenty of speed for a motherboard, at least through the year 2000. The peripherals communicate with the CPU at 33MHz, anyway, and the memory that can keep up with this rate is expensive. On the newest motherboards, the drive can communicate with the CPU at 66MHz. This is made possible by the VIA 82XXX chip, so make sure the motherboard supports 66MHz EIDE connections. The board won't be inexpensive, but it will make the most of your hard drives.

In our experience, you don't need the fastest CPU on the market. The fastest will become the second fastest the moment you bring it home (and it costs a small fortune). So go for the preceding-generation CPU. Today, the fastest CPUs run at 700MHz, approximately, and 500MHz to 600MHz Pentiums are a very good deal. Next year you will probably replace it, so don't go overboard on your choice of CPU. By the time you read this book, the 700MHz CPU may be a good deal, as the fastest CPUs will be running very close to 1GHz.

Try to purchase a motherboard that comes with the CPU—many do, and they cost about the same as purchasing them separately. Otherwise, buy them both from the same vendor so that you can return them both if there's a problem.

Most motherboards accept up to 512KB of external cache—but they come with 128KB of cache memory. Purchase the additional cache memory with the motherboard. If you're going to mail-order the motherboard, ask that the cache memory be preinstalled.

Hard Drives

This is where your data (in other words, your livelihood) will be stored. Buy a reliable hard drive that's larger than you need. Capacities of 10–20GB are commonplace today, so go for a really large drive. The price differential is such that anything less than 10GB isn't a great deal—for 25% more you can get twice the capacity. I'm assuming you'll install Windows on the new computer, so you won't have to worry about the 2.1GB limit of DOS.

In terms of speed, consider a UDMA (Ultra Direct Memory Access) 66MHz hard drive. If you go for this drive, make sure the motherboard can support this speed. When comparing models, remember that higher transfer and burst rates are better.

In our opinion, two drives are better than one. What are the chances of two drives dying on you at once? You can actually use part of the second drive to back up your most useful data. It's wise to equip the new computer with a backup device, as well, but with today's disk prices, you can use a hard drive as a backup unit.

Floppy Drives

OK, this is probably the simplest peripheral to shop for. Get a 3½" drive so that you can start your computer from a floppy, or install a device that comes with diskettes only—many network cards, for example, come with an installation diskette.

Floppies were used to exchange files with other users. If the files are more than a few MB, the medium of choice is a Zip disk. You can get both internal and external Zip drives; and you should opt for the internal one because it's faster. Most people have access to a Zip drive, either in their office or at home, which makes it an extremely useful peripheral. When the Zip drive first appeared, people were buying external Zip drives so that they could take their data (along with the drive) anywhere. Nowadays, Zip drives are approaching everyday status.

Most users exchange files electronically and the floppy drive is for the most part a thing of the past. The only reason you need a floppy drive is because you may have to start up the computer with a floppy (the Windows Emergency floppy, for instance, or the Rescue floppies of your antivirus software). We have a notebook with a removable floppy drive and a LAN/modem card, and we probably haven't used the floppy more than once or twice. Probably the best substitute is the SuperDrive, which can read and write 1.4MB diskettes but can also handle 120MB diskettes. Since no desktop computer can be without a floppy drive, get a SuperDrive and let it double as a floppy drive (and then you can restart your dream computer with the emergency diskette—God forbid!).

The Video Board and Monitor

Modern software relies heavily on graphics; even the operating system is a visual environment. Go for an advanced video board with built-in 3D graphics and rendering capabilities, and lots of memory. The best video card standard today is AGP. This board has its own processor and can display stunning graphics and mind-boggling animation. Buy an AGP card with as much memory as you can afford, because the card will make your dream computer shine. Keep in mind that the more video memory on the card, the higher resolution you can achieve; but a color depth of 16 million colors is more than your eyes can discern. Buy enough memory so that the video card can display 16 million colors at a resolution of 1024×768.

An expensive video card deserves a good monitor, don't you think? Actually, your eyes deserve a good monitor even more. Go for a 17-inch monitor with a very high refresh rate. A 15-inch monitor is too small for today's resolutions, but the 19-inch monitor is too big for a typical desk. You shouldn't scrimp on the monitor, because it's the one part that can't be easily replaced. Monitors are expensive, and selling your used one won't bring you much.

The most important monitor specification is the refresh rate. Don't buy a monitor that doesn't support a refresh rate of 100Hz or more, at 1024×768. If you're buying a 19-inch monitor, you can use it with a higher resolution, say 1280×1024. Make sure that even at the highest resolution, the monitor supports a refresh rate of 100Hz. A crucial, but often overlooked, monitor specification is its size. A 19-inch monitor won't fit nicely on a small desk and you may have to work too close to the monitor. Don't buy a 21-inch monitor unless you need a very high resolution and you have a desk that can accommodate it.

CD-ROM/DVD Drive

A CD-ROM is another device you can't be without. All software now comes on CD-ROM and in the near future it will be available on DVDs. Your first choice should be the DVD drive, unless you're sure you won't be watching movies on your computer. A DVD drive will read regular CD-ROMs, so you'll be able to use all of your CDs with it.

Also make sure that the DVD drive supports hardware decompression. The hardware decoder produces the sharpest possible image, so avoid DVD drives with software decoders. The fastest DVD drives today are 6X–8X (some even faster by the time you read this), and when they read CDs they're as fast as a 20X CD-ROM drive. If you want to be able to write your own CDs (to back up large files, for example), you need a CD-R in addition to the DVD drive.

The Modem

In our day and age, a good modem is a must. The fastest modem speed you can buy is 56Kbps. Buy an internal one because it's considerably less expensive than an external one. If you want an external modem (perhaps you like to watch the LEDs), consider one with a USB connection.

Even the fastest modem, however, is not fast enough for the Internet. An ISDN or ADSL connection is much faster and not terribly expensive (prices continue to drop). Buy a modem that works everywhere, and consult with the ISPs in your area to find out what other options you have. They will provide all the necessary hardware for the connection. This hardware is usually a box that looks like a modem and connects to the serial or USB port, but it's not really a modem.

Exercise

Assuming that you have purchased all the parts, here are the steps for putting them together. To make the procedure more manageable, we've divided it into two broad stages, but you may be able to complete it in one session.

To Install and Test the CPU and Memory

1. Remove the case's cover to get to the interior. Find out where everything goes, identify the screws that hold it in place, and visualize the case after it has been filled with the parts.

2. See how the motherboard fits in the case. The motherboard must be oriented so that its EIDE connectors are near the front of the case (where the drive bays are located), and the ports are near the back of the case. Locate the screws and spacers that will hold the motherboard in place and set them aside.

3. Before you place the motherboard in the case, insert the CPU and the memory, and set the jumpers accordingly.

4. If the CPU is not already on the motherboard, insert the CPU in the special socket. This will be a ZIF socket or a slot. If it's a ZIF socket, lift the lever, align the notch on the CPU with the notch on the socket, place the CPU in the socket, and push the lever down to hold the CPU in place.

5. Most modern motherboards accept an SEC CPU. Just align the contacts of the CPU to the slot and insert it smoothly.

6. If the CPU has its own fan, there will be a short power cable attached to the CPU. The other end of the cable is a Berg connector. Locate a small connector on the motherboard near the CPU and use it to connect the power cable from the CPU.

7. If you have any cache memory modules to install on the motherboard, do it now. Cache memory is a single chip, which you must insert in the proper socket on the motherboard (see the motherboard's documentation for the location).

8. Now set the jumpers to reflect the speed of the CPU. If the motherboard came with the CPU on it, the jumpers are set, but it wouldn't hurt to verify their settings.

9. Use the motherboard's documentation to find out the location of the clock multiplier's jumpers, and set them accordingly. If the motherboard doesn't have a group of jumpers for the multiplier, don't worry. You'll be able to set the multiplier from within the BIOS Setup program.

10. Next, set the voltage jumpers according to the voltage required by the CPU. Consult the documentation and set these jumpers correctly, or else you may destroy the CPU. If the CPU comes with the motherboard, the jumpers are already set for you (another reason to purchase a motherboard with a CPU on it). If the motherboard doesn't have a group of jumpers for the voltage, don't worry. You'll be able to set the proper voltage from within the BIOS Setup program.

11. Insert the memory modules into their slots. The memory modules are always DIMMs, and you need one module per bank. If the motherboard has dual memory banks, be sure to fill both banks, or else the computer won't see the memory.

12. Now you can attach the motherboard to the case. Consult the documentation, use all the spacers that came with the case, and screw the motherboard firmly on the chassis. The screws that hold the motherboard to the chassis have washers too. Make sure you use them. (Many motherboards are held in place by the spacers and don't require screws.)

13. Place the video card into one of the slots. If you have a motherboard with its own graphics board and you're installing a video card, make sure you disable the on-board video card.

14. You're almost ready to test the motherboard, CPU, and memory. If the power supply isn't already attached to the case, attach it now. Chances are the power supply is already mounted on the chassis, and all you'll have to do is connect a few wires to the motherboard.

15. Plug the cables that come out of the power supply into the motherboard. There should be a large Molex connector that fits the motherboard's power connector. If the motherboard has two power connectors, you must connect a power cable to each one (see Labs 6 and 10 for more information).

16. Attach the monitor's VGA cable to the video board's connector, plug in the power cable, and turn on the monitor.

17. Now turn on the computer. You'll see the BIOS message on the monitor, followed by the usual memory count. Then the BIOS will say something to the effect that it can't find a disk. Turn the computer off.

18. If you can't see anything on the monitor, make sure the video board is connected properly and it's working. Do you have an Energy Saving monitor? When the computer is off, the monitor's LED will be yellow. As soon as you turn on the computer, this LED will turn green. If it doesn't, it's not accepting any signal from the computer. See if the power supply is working (you should hear the fan); if it works, double-check the installation of the video card and monitor connection. If the computer came on and it saw the correct amount of memory, you can continue by installing the drives.

To Install the Hard Drives and CD-ROM

Assuming you've been able to turn on the computer and start the BIOS, you're ready to install the drives.

1. Turn off the computer and disconnect the power cables. You're probably using an APM motherboard, which doesn't have a real power switch, so you can't cut off power completely. Unplug the power cord from the power outlet.

2. Insert the floppy drive's data cable to the floppy drive and then a power cable to the floppy drive's power connector. You have no reason to use two floppy drives on this machine, so plug the other end of the floppy cable to the floppy connector on the motherboard. Then insert the floppy drive in its bay and screw it on. If you have access to the case's interior from the top, place the floppy in the lowest bay.

3. Now connect the other data cable (the one that came with the hard drive) to the hard drive. If you have two drives, use a data cable with two connectors at the end.

4. The other end of the hard drive's data cable must go to the primary EIDE connector on the motherboard (it's marked as EIDE1, Disk1, or something similar).

5. If you have two drives, don't forget to set the jumpers on one of them in the slave position. If you have a hard drive and CD-ROM, connect them to different EIDE connectors on the motherboard. If you configure the CD-ROM as a slave device and connect it to the same connector as the hard drive, when you move data between the hard disk and the CD-ROM, the transfer will take place at the rate of the CD-ROM.

6. Plug a power cable into each drive and insert the drives into their bays.

7. Now you're ready to start the computer and see if the BIOS recognizes the drives. Attach the mouse and the keyboard, plug the power cord into the outlet, and turn on the computer.

8. Press the appropriate key(s) to enter the BIOS Setup program.

9. The STANDARD CMOS SETUP screen should list all the drives, and indicate whether they're on the primary or secondary connector, and which one is the master drive. If the BIOS hasn't recognized the drives, you'll have to either key in the characteristics of the drives or ask the BIOS to auto-detect them. But first double-check the connections and the jumpers on the drives; chances are you haven't wired the drives correctly. If all is well, go ahead and attempt to auto-detect them.

10. While you're in the STANDARD CMOS SETUP screen, set the date and time. Then set the startup sequence (it should be drive C and then drive A). If the multiplier must be set from within the BIOS setup program, do so now.

11. We're almost there. Turn off the computer one last time, open the case (if you've closed it), and install the CD-ROM drive. Attach the CD-ROM (or DVD) drive to the secondary controller on the motherboard. If you have to place the CD-ROM on the same cable as another drive, set the CD-ROM drive as slave.

NOTE If you want to install Windows directly from the CD-ROM, make the CD-ROM the master device in its connector. Later, set it as the boot device in the BIOS.

---

12. If you have an internal modem, insert it into one of the available slots, screw it on, and you're done.

13. Turn the computer on and insert the Windows installation CD in the CD-ROM drive. Watch the BIOS recognize the drives, count the memory, and then start the Windows installation program. If the CD-ROM is not the boot device, use a diskette to boot and then the Windows 98 CD to install the operating system. After you've installed the operating system, you can start the BIOS Setup program and make one of the hard drives the boot device.

Lab 40

DATE _____ NAME _____

1. Draw a diagram of the new motherboard. Identify the IDE connectors, the multiplier's jumpers, and the voltage jumpers. Write down the settings of the jumpers.

    _____

    _____

    _____

    _____

    _____

2. Write down the specifications of the hard drive(s) and how they're connected to the motherboard (primary/secondary, master/slave).

    _____

    _____

    _____

    _____

    _____

    _____

3. How are the CPU speed, bus speed, and memory speed related? If you had a faster bus on the motherboard, how would it affect the performance of the computer?

_____

_____

_____

_____

_____

_____

Appendix: Six Essential Upgrades

- **Removing and Installing SDRAM Modules**

- **Installing a New Power Supply**

- **Installing an EIDE Hard Drive**

- **Installing a Video Card**

- **Installing a Sound Card**

- **Installing a DVD Drive**

Visual Upgrade: Removing and Installing SDRAM Modules

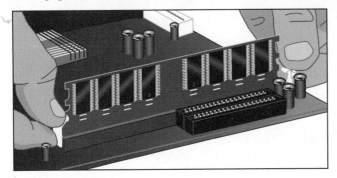

1 Pull the plastic clips at both ends of the slot away from the SDRAM module.

2 Gently pull the SDRAM module from the slot on the motherboard.

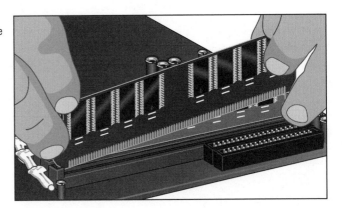

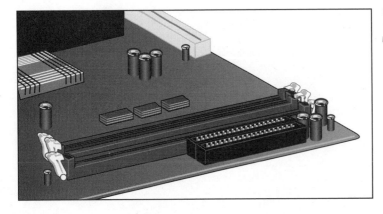

3 A motherboard with all of the SDRAM memory modules removed.

 Carefully insert new SDRAM memory modules into the slot.

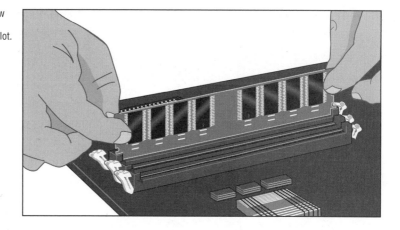

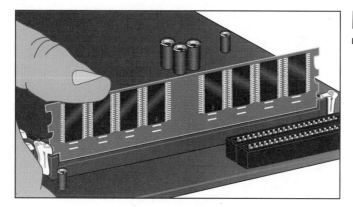

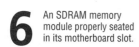 Press the SDRAM memory module into the slot until the plastic clips lock. (If it doesn't snap into place, press the lever inward.)

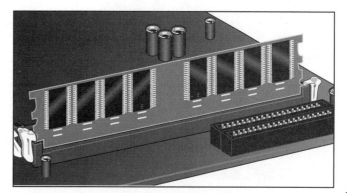 An SDRAM memory module properly seated in its motherboard slot.

Visual Upgrade: Installing a New Power Supply

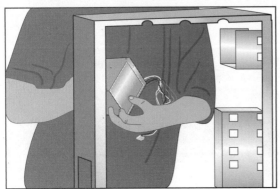

1 Position the new power supply unit at the rear of the case.

2 Fasten the power supply to the chassis with four screws.

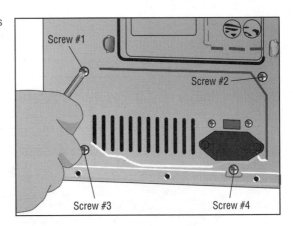

Screw #1

Screw #2

Screw #3

Screw #4

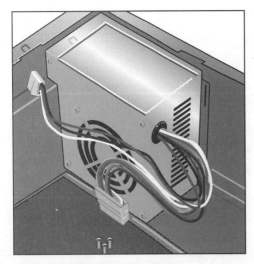

3 Connect the power supply's largest connectors to the motherboard. The connectors are keyed so that you cannot connect them incorrectly.

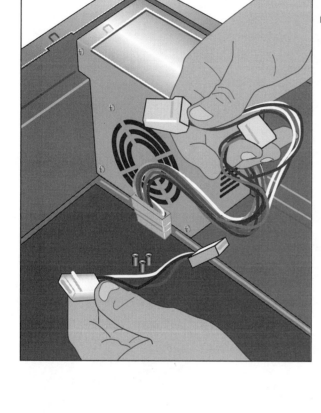

4 Connect the other Molex and Berg connectors to the fan, hard and floppy drives, CD-ROM drive, etc.

5 Plug the computer's power cord into the new power supply unit.

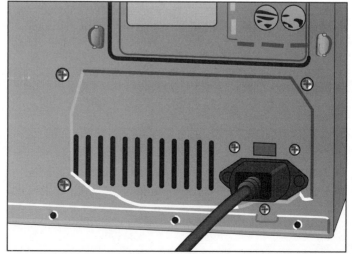

269

Visual Upgrade: Installing an EIDE Hard Drive

1 Mount the new drive in the computer chassis (or removable drive bay). Be sure to use two screws on each side!

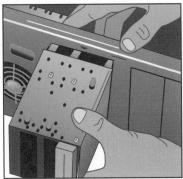

2 If the computer has a removable drive bay, mount it into the computer's chassis and lock it into place.

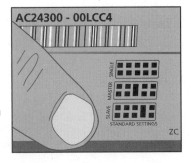

3 Check the drive's documentation (either in the manual or on the drive itself) for the drive's master/slave settings.

4 Set the jumper at the rear of the drive to signify either master or slave status.

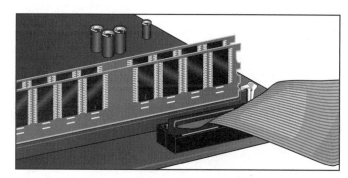

5 Connect the drive data cable to the EIDE connector on the motherboard (if you are installing the first or third EIDE in the computer).

6 Connect the free end of the EIDE data cable into the connector at the rear of the hard drive.

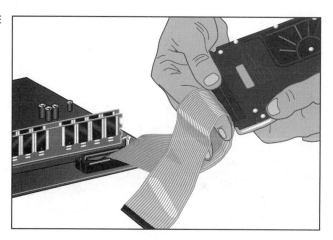

7 Connect the power supply's Molex plug into the power connector at the rear of the hard drive.

Molex plug

Visual Upgrade: Installing a Video Card

1 Never handle a circuit board by its edge connector; oils from your fingers can cause connectivity problems.

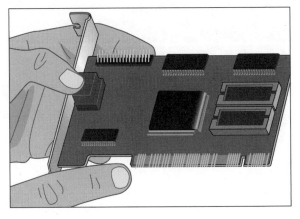

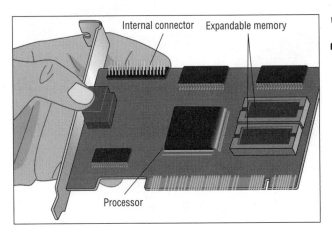

Internal connector   Expandable memory

Processor

2 Most video cards have expandable memory, a processor, and an internal connector.

3 The internal connector on a video card is called a feature connector; most commonly it is used to connect a television tuner or other video device to the computer's video card.

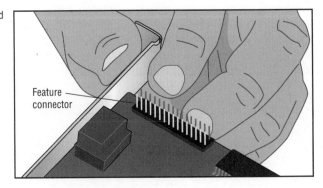

Feature connector

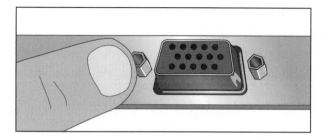

4 A video card's 15-pin, D-shell connector is the standard plug for all computer video monitors.

5 Align the video card with the slot and press it down until it clicks into place.

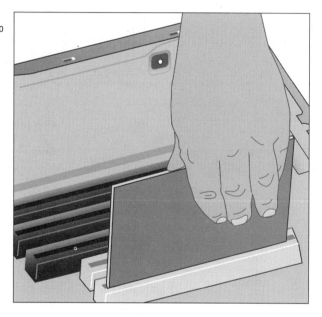

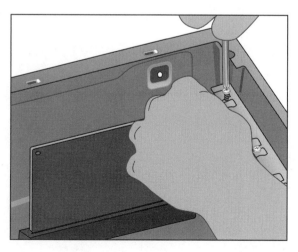

6 Mount the card securely by screwing the video card's rear plate into the computer's chassis.

Visual Upgrade: Installing a Sound Card

1 Sound cards have several internal and external connectors.

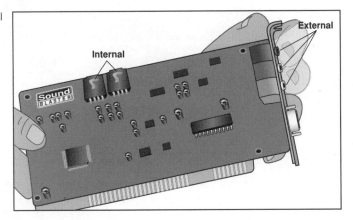

2 The rear of most sound cards has a joystick port in addition to mini-plug jacks for speakers, line in, and a microphone.

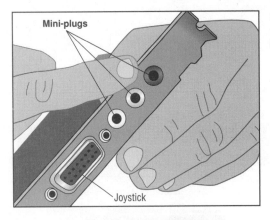

3 Insert the sound card into a free slot (ISA or PCI, depending on the type of card).

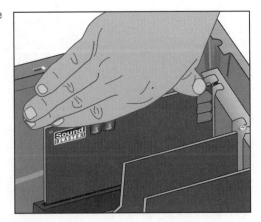

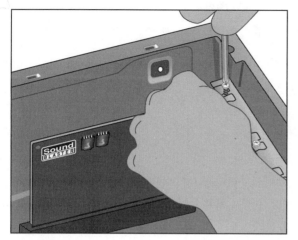

4 Screw the back plate of the card into the computer's chassis.

5 Connect one end of your CD-ROM's audio cable into the internal CD IN connector on the sound card.

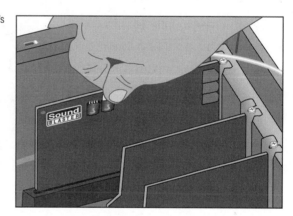

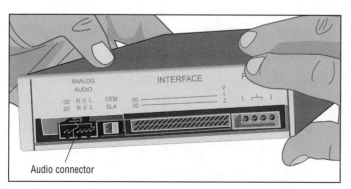

Audio connector

6 Connect the other end of the audio cable to the AUDIO connector at the rear of the CD-ROM drive.

Visual Upgrade: Installing a DVD Drive

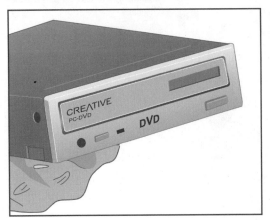

1 Install an internal DVD drive into an open 5-1/4" drive bay in your computer.

2 Most DVD drives use a hardware decoder board that must be installed in an open PCI slot.

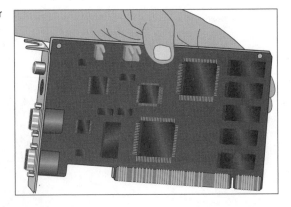

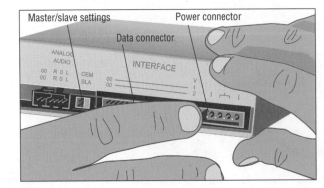

3 The rear of the DVD drive has several areas: the master/slave settings at the left; the data connector in the center; and the power connector at the right.

4 After setting the master/slave jumper, connect the IDE data cable to the drive. Then connect the power connector to the drive.

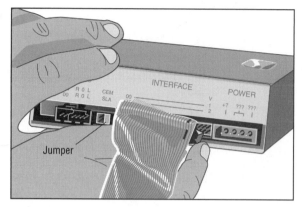

Jumper

5 The DVD decoder card has two video connectors: one for input and one for output.

Decoder Video In

System Video Out

Decoder Video Out

6 Attach a loopback cable from the computer video board's Video Out connector to the DVD decoder's Video In connector. Then connect your monitor's video cable to the DVD decoder board's Video Out connector.

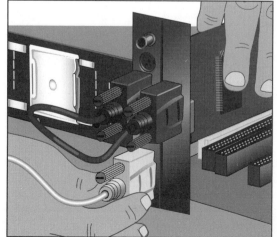

277

Notes

Notes

Notes